Modernization in Ghana and the U.S.S.R.

A Comparative Study

by Robert E. Dowse
Department of Government
University of Exeter

LONDON
ROUTLEDGE & KEGAN PAUL
NEW YORK: HUMANITIES PRESS

First published 1969
by Routledge & Kegan Paul Ltd
Broadway House, 68–74 Carter Lane
London E.C.4

Printed in Great Britain
by Willmer Brothers Limited
Birkenhead, Cheshire

SBN 7100 6171 4

General Editor's introduction

This series of monographs is designed primarily to meet the needs of students of government, politics, or political science in Universities and other institutions providing courses leading to degrees. Each volume aims to provide a brief general introduction indicating the significance of its topic e.g. executives, parties, pressure groups, etc., and then a longer 'case study' relevant to the general topic. First year students will thus be introduced to the kind of detailed work on which all generalizations must be based, while more mature students will have an opportunity to become acquainted with recent original research in a variety of fields. The series will eventually provide a comprehensive coverage of most aspects of political science in a more interesting and fundamental manner than in the large volume which often fails to compensate by breadth what it inevitably lacks in depth.

Robert Dowse, who has previously published in the fields of political parties and comparative methodology, attempts in this volume to draw a number of comparisons between political developments in Soviet Russia and in Ghana. Party systems, ideologies, the structure of the two countries, combine with the 'logic of the situation' to produce the political patterns referred to in this monograph. The foci of the study have been drawn from a wide range of contemporary American comparative schemes. Limitations of space unfortunately precluded a proper discussion of a number of basic theoretical considerations. Not the least of these considerations concerns the problem of comparability between systems as apparently different as those of Ghana and the U.S.S.R. In a future volume Dr Dowse will discuss some of the problems of comparability at length.

H.V.W.

CONTENTS

CONTENTS

This volume is a study of some aspects of the politics of modernization in two states, the U.S.S.R. and Ghana. One of the major contentions of this volume is that they faced a variety of similar problems and that their responses to these had a great deal in common. For example the most obvious similarity between the two was the single-party state with a relatively high degree of control exercised by the party leadership over the party. There are also a large number of striking similarities concerning attitudes to economic development and the outside world.

The most important problem that had to be solved in both states was that of economic development. Perhaps this should be phrased differently: the problem that most concerned the new leaders of Ghana and Russia was that of economic development. Political priorities were assessed in the light or by the standard of systems of ideas, of ideologies. Hence, we will have to examine the development of these ideas. However, the overall thesis of the volume is that although Marxism-Leninism and Nkrumaism differ greatly, the leaders of the two countries in fact behaved in a remarkably similar fashion. That is, their responses had as much to do with similar problems as with ideological patterns.

The basic proposition of the book is that in an under-developed country the range of possible economic and political strategies open to the leaders is relatively narrow. By definition the resources which make options relatively open are not available. If, on top of this, the political élite determines upon—for any reason—a tactic of rapid industrialization it is likely to impose massive burdens on the population.

To
Peter and Sheila

1
The background

In both the U.S.S.R. and Ghana the single-party systems
arose from what might be called a crisis situation; in
Russia defeat in war followed by Allied intervention
against a background of a devastated economy and empire crumbling into its constituent units. The Ghanian
crisis was by no means as dramatic and obvious as in the
case of Russia. In 1957 the new country of Ghana appeared on the brink of collapsing into its three or four
major socio-geographic entities. Looked at from the point
of view of the leadership of the Convention Peoples Party
(C.P.P.), and the Communist Party (C.P.) both of which
were strongly centralist, the great adventures began in
difficult circumstances. Given that the leadership wished
to hold their countries together what alternatives had
they? And what were the major weapons in the armoury
of centralist unification?

But if there were serious problems of national unification, it is equally true that the problem, or rather problems, of building a modern economy were also urgent
and pressing. Both countries were, by any standards,
seriously underdeveloped. That is, they lacked an economic and social infra-structure appropriate to modern
industrial and administrative needs. Schools, hospitals,

universities, roads, railways and communications were in a relatively poor state. Lacking these facilities was one thing, but far far more important was what one might call psychological or attitudinal under-development. Attitudes to saving and investing, to the family, to obligation, to regularity, etc., were not such as to encourage the widespread initiative which underpins economic development. Given the need for rapid political and industrial development what range of alternatives was open to the leadership in both countries to bring about the all-important attitudinal revolution? And what sort of basis was available to them for building up the administrative, technical and communications infra-structure?

Education

It has already been claimed that the educational basis for building a modern state was weak in both Ghana and Russia; let us look at the picture more closely. By African standards Ghanaian educational achievements by the 1950's were high with a total enrolment in primary education of some 281,000 representing 6.6% of the total population, but of these only 1% went on to secondary schools. This represented a substantial increase over the 1920 figure when only some 42,300 were in the primary and secondary schools, most of the increase taking place since 1945 (Foster, 1965). Not until 1948 was a university education available in the country, although considerable numbers of Africans had obtained advanced education overseas. In addition, although education carried high prestige, 'the modern specialist's engineering degree counts for less than the classical British traditions of scholarship' (Apter, 1955, 63).

Russian educational facilities prior to 1917 for the masses were similarly poor with 76% of the population illiterate and only 20% receiving any education; but about 20% of those in elementary schools went on to secondary schools (Maxwell, 1962). Russian university education in 1914 was relatively impressive with ten universities catering for some 62,000 students and about 105 'higher educational establishments'. As in Ghana, a considerable amount of Russian primary and secondary education was provided by voluntary associations such as churches. Also, as in Ghana, the impact of educational opportunity varied greatly from area to area. Russian secondary education displayed a strong leaning towards classics, especially in the Gymnasiums where boys were prepared for the universities.

Politics

Although in 1914 Russia was economically backward it had advanced with great rapidity; and it was a formidable European economic power being Europe's largest oil producer, third in machine construction and the fourth largest producer of steel. It was the fifth most powerful industrial nation in the world (Maxwell, 1962). In addition, its agricultural sector accounted for about 51% of total production with industry accounting for some 28%. Productivity, volume of savings, foreign investments, size of the industrial unit, percentage of age of working population etc. had all dramatically increased between 1900–1913 (Lyashchenko, 1949). It is not without significance that, as in Ghana, a very considerable percentage of Russian industry, extractive and manufacturing, was controlled by external investors. Agriculture too was being modernized with the Stolypin land reforms of 1906 which encouraged peasants to opt out of the older communal pattern of ownership and farming and become individual land-owning cultivators. By 1916 about 24% of households in European Russia personally held their lands.

Politically Russia advanced a trifle towards a representative system of government with the 1906 reforms and a very modest measure of local government reform was introduced in 1909. The Emperor retained massive reserve powers, but something was conceded. In the 1906 elections the government was decisively defeated with the Constitutional Democrats obtaining 38% of deputies and the Left about 25%. This Duma was dissolved and further elections in 1907 produced a polarization, with Left and Right gaining at the expense of the centre. Soon even these grudged changes were whittled away. But at the administrative level Russia remained an almost total chaos without even the limited reforms that had affected the Duma. The bureaucracy was immense and inefficient and had apparently changed little in over a generation (Walsh, 1958).

By 1914, then, Russia had advanced considerably in terms of production; its educational system, although poor by West European standards was improving and by no means negligible. Only in the political system did it lag seriously in the sense of making few marked advances and its bureaucracy was corrupt and grossly inefficient. The war was to demonstrate quite how unsuited to serious strain the political and administrative arrangements were. By 1916 they had almost totally collapsed. And during the civil war Russian industrial production dropped by more than 80%.

Ghana in 1957 differed in many ways from the Russian pattern—its major advance had been in the political system although the economy was developing relatively quickly. British rule in the Gold Coast for the most part was indirect through the native authorities; although ultimately detrimental to the traditional authority of Gold Coast chiefs the effect of the policy was to bring them within the ambit of government and to give them some experience of modern administration. Similarly, the British, albeit apparently reluctantly, had by 1951 initiated a range of political reform making possible the incorporation of the local élites into the governmental apparatus both central and local. Discussing the period up to 1948 Austin rightly claims that under the Governor, Sir Allen Burns, reforms 'amounted to a bold attempt to meet any widespread demand for political rights before it reached the point of violent controversy' (Austin, 1964, 9). For example, the Coussey Commission—composed entirely of Africans—reported in October 1949 and recommended a semi-responsible executive with an unofficial majority together with a legislative assembly nationally elected. The Report was accepted almost in its entirety by the British and the effect was to bring the whole adult population directly into the constitutional arena as legal participants.

Administrative improvement on the Gold Coast also proceeded with reasonable despatch. The general trend was, although painfully slow, towards bringing Africans into the administrative structure at all levels. Economic progress had also been rapid, although the diversification of the economy had hardly begun. Thus in 1935 cocoa represented 56% of total exports and in 1950 it was 75%.

But when this has been said on the credit side for the old regimes—those preceeding Lenin and Nkrumah—an enormous effort was necessary if they were to be thrust rapidly into economic and political modernity. In both countries the efficiency of labour was extremely low, the general level of health was poor, communications were primitive, attitudes to work and time generally pre-

5

industrial and neither country was securely unified. All this needed changing, and if the evidence suggests that they were changing prior to the 'revolutions', the revolutions are also evidence that they were not changing fast enough!

The C.P.P. and the Communist Party

In both countries the instrument of change was the political party: and in both countries the party was a radical or activist offshoot of a larger more 'moderate' political party. Nkrumah, like Lenin, clearly attached great importance to organization and had been a founder member of The Circle in London which was based upon the idea that 'no movement can endure unless there is a stable organization of trained, selected and trusted men to maintain continuity'. Nkrumah's break with the United Gold Coast Convention was a break by a more highly organized and professional political elite from a group less highly organized. No serious differences of immediate programme were evident since both U.G.C.C. and C.P.P. were demanding rapid self-government. What intellectual differences there were appeared to be as much temperamental as ideological. But from his appointment as U.G.C.C. secretary in December 1947 Nkrumah took the lead in *organizing* the party for effective political agitation. By January 1948 he had called a meeting of the U.G.C.C. working committee and presented them with a plan of action heavily stressing the need for organized political activity: policy was not mentioned (Nkrumah, 1959). Nkrumah, at least was reluctant to take the differences between his section of the U.G.C.C. and that of the more moderate constitutionalists to a final split. It was popular pressure from below that finally nerved him to secede, in June 1949, and form the C.P.P.

6

This was not the case with Lenin's organizational split from the Russian Social Democratic Labour Party in 1912. Indeed, from at least 1903 Lenin was consciously planning and manoeuvring a split on the twin issues of a tight party membership and intellectual monolithism. There were deep temperamental differences between Lenin and Nkrumah—one an unbending puritan pedagogue and the other a vacillating rather timid man—but on the issue of the central importance of organizaion they were one.

There were emotional differences between the two men, but it is likely that environmental differences were more significant in the eventual outcome of their respective revolutions. It is fashionable to argue that the British colonial regime on the Gold Coast was authoritarian, and in many respects it was, but in contrast to the Romanov regime that of the British was mildly liberal. The press was free—within the limits of libel laws—and voluntary associations were positively encouraged; there was no equivalent of Okhrana, and the West African Siberia was mild! We have yet to find evidence of *agents provocateurs* in Ghana working under police direction: Lenin's secretary was a police spy. In fact, the political atmosphere of the Gold Coast was not such as to throw up a revolutionary intransigent on the Leninist model. Lenin was in many ways an inverted copy of the Russia of the 1890's and 1900's. And Nkrumah *needed* to be little more than a pale copy of Lenin. At least in terms of achieving independence any more would have been a waste. But the same was not true of the post-independence epoch when, given Nkrumah's desire for a rapidly industrializing society, a Lenin or a Stalin might have been more appropriate.

7

Organizing theories

Lenin's organizational thesis was first elaborated in 1902 in the long pamphlet *What is to be Done?* In part a bitter polemic against other factions of parties, and a serious revision of Marx's spontaneity, it is mainly a plea for a tightly controlled and rigidly organized revolutionary party. The heart of the argument is as follows:

(1) No revolutionary movement can endure without a stable organization of leaders that maintains continuity;

(2) the wider the masses spontaneously drawn into the struggle, forming the basis of the movement and participating in it, the more urgent the need of such an organization, and the more solid this organization must be;

(3) such an organization must consist chiefly of people professionally engaged in revolutionary activity.

The functions of the organized and disciplined party for both Nkrumah and Lenin were simple: to educate the masses in socialist/nationalist consciousness in order that they would be able to see through the blandishments of other parties and moderates. In Nkrumah's words 'This type of education should do away with the kind of intelligentsia who have become the very architects of colonial enslavement' (Nkrumah, 1947, 36). The party was to be a kind of guardian, in the case of Lenin actually to *bring* to the masses the message of salvation and in Nkrumah's case to prevent 'demagogues, quislings, traitors, cowards and self-seekers to lead astray any section of the masses of the African people' (Timothy, 1963, 52). Although there is a difference in the formulation, it is quite clear that for both the political party was to play a vital rôle in their respective political milieus. In Shils' useful phrase, both

8

parties possessed very strongly a 'sense of exclusive cus-
todianship of the national essence'.

But the rôle of the party was not confined simply to
that of guardianship, it had also to usher in social and
economic reconstruction. Since the very foundation of
the marxist theory of social development was rooted in
industrialism and its progress it followed that Lenin and
the Russian Social Democrats had to tackle the problem
of Russia's backwardness. Marx, although allowing the
possibility of agrarian socialism in Russia, had originally
envisaged that socialism would arrive first in the more
developed countries; should the Russian socialists then
remain passive, awaiting economic and political developments, or should they give history a push? That is, at its
crudest, should political 'adventurism' replace economic
development as the mainspring of history? Lenin's answer
to this was unequivocal. An alliance of proletariat and
peasantry—led by the party vanguard—could bring about
a political revolution upon which could be based a subsequent socialist transformation. Thus the hub of Leninism
was the primacy of *Politics*. From the very fact of Russia's
economic backwardness Lenin drew the conclusion that the
way forward was a political revolution which would give
the party a vantage point from which to lever the economy
into rapid socialist advance.

That Kwame Nkrumah had read Lenin on Imperialism is
quite clear from his 1947 pamphlet, *Towards Colonial
Freedom*. For Nkrumah, 'The object of the Imperialist
Powers is to exploit. By granting the right to the Colonial
peoples to govern themselves, they are defeating that objective. Therefore, the struggle for political power by Colonial
and subject people is the first step towards, and the necessary prerequisite to, complete social economic and political emancipation'. As with Lenin so with Nkrumah:

9

political power was a necessary prerequisite to social revolution.

Another significant parallel between the ideas of the two party leaders also concerns politics, but this time foreign politics. Both envisaged their own revolutions not simply as the end of a political process but rather as the beginning of a wider chain of events. Neither believed that internal political and economic advance was enough, both wished to operate on a pan-national scale. From well before he achieved any significance on the Gold Coast Nkrumah was an ardent advocate of West African unity claiming that 'unless territorial freedom was ultimately linked up with the Pan-African movement for the liberation of the whole of the African continent, there would be no hope of freedom and equality for the African' (Nkrumah, 1959). At this stage in his career the intellectual underpinnings for this belief were flimsy, but he later explained and analysed the necessity for political union in a series of books and speeches. Bolshevik belief in an active foreign policy was much more intellectually coherent.

From at least the 1848 Communist Manifesto it was an article of faith that workers were without nationality or patriotism and that their real interests and allegiance lay with the international proletariat rather than the nation state. Hence, the first socialist state would win the allegiance of the international proletariat. For the Bolsheviks there was another consideration. If a revolution first occurred in Russia it would be abortive unless supported from the more economically developed countries of the West. The belief was that Germany, the most socially advanced of European countries, would have its socialist revolution and in a spirit of socialist internationalism create a Russian economic base.

Soviet internationalism and Pan-Africanism, at least Nkrumah's version of it, however, very rapidly met with serious external resistance and led to the isolation of Ghana and contributed to that of the U.S.S.R. Russian policy remained, in words at least, dominated by ideas of proletarian internationalism, but on the more practical level 'the primacy of domestic power considerations established in the discussion over Brest-Litovsk has remained paramount in Soviet foreign policy decisions' (Rostow, 1954). Nkrumah, on the other hand, appears to have become more and more pre-occupied with African and foreign politics, and it was hardly a coincidence that he was replaced whilst engaged upon a 'diplomatic' mission. Stopping off to meet President Nasser, 'Nkrumah said he wanted to talk about Vietnam. I (Nasser) said no, please let us talk about Ghana ... But it was no use; he did not seem worried at all' (*Guardian*, 27.4.66).

The significance of the external vision is clear. It provides a built-in dynamism; political interest and involvement does not stop at the frontiers and is not confined to normal diplomatic relations. The object of foreign policy is not simply to change other countries' policies, but rather to change the context of policy. Such an object is likely to arouse deep suspicion of the motives of those pursuing the policy, and equally clearly such a suspicion can easily harden into enmity. Such soon became the case in both the U.S.S.R. and Ghana.

The leadership of both parties then was committed to organizational and political ideas that have some significant measure of comparability and the situations they faced had many striking similarities. What then of the parties they built and controlled? And is there any comparability of patterns of support for the two parties?

Structure of support

Both the C.P.P. and the C.P. were thoroughly committed to fundamental social change—and hence attracted primarily those social groups most alienated from the existing situation. Note, for example, the numbers in the Executive of both parties who were 'Prison Graduates'. Also in the C.P. the strong minority representation from Balts, Finns and Jews. Again, the Bolsheviks regarded the Romanov's and indeed Russian institutions as somehow alien, and indeed a great deal of Russian industry was foreign-owned. The Russian and Ghanaian revolutions, like the French, saw the dropping away of middle-class progressives as it became evident that the drift of the revolutions was not to stop at political reform—to replace one élite by another similar one—but would proceed towards far-reaching social reform. Dealers in words and ideas predominated at the top of the parties, whilst below membership was socially more disparate. In the C.P.P. 'Cadres for this party were largely drawn from new middle-class elements ... But the rank and file were drawn from the peasants, the workers and, most importantly, the market-women' (Wallerstein, 1964). But the top educational and intellectual level was below that of a similar level in the C.P. Moreover in both parties, from top to bottom, the membership was new to 'legal' politics with the extravagant hopes and aspirations of such people. In this way they resembled the French revolutionaries, and the Fascists and the Nazis.

However, although both countries were primarily agricultural the C.P.P. was more successful than was the C.P. in mobilizing support in the non-urban areas 'Organized primarily in the towns the C.P.P., with the assistance of lorry and taxi drivers, railway workers, market-women, teachers and "standard vii boys", shop-keepers and others spread into the villages' (Coleman and Rosberg, 1964, 271). The Communists never made any serious impact at all on the villages, having only 7.6% of a total membership of 23,600 from peasant backgrounds (Fainsod, 1953). But it must be kept firmly in mind that both parties were primarily urban political parties in overwhelmingly rural countries. Not only this, they were also parties of the young; in 1950 C.P.P. average age in the Legislative Assembly was 35.8 years and on the central committee of the C.P. in 1925 more than 86% were under 50 years old.

Bolshevism from its origins had been highly urbanized and despite Lenin's 'Two Tactics' its whole intellectual orientation was towards the working class representing, as it did, the socialist future. What strength the party had lay in the factories and the unions, whilst in the countryside it was practically unknown (Maynard, 1962). That this was so is evident from Russia's first and last free election for a Constituent Assembly in November 1917 when the Bolsheviks received 25% of votes cast. The Socialist Revolutionaries overwhelmingly received the peasant vote—non-Bolshevik Socialists obtaining about 62% of votes cast—and the Bolshevik vote was concentrated largely in Petrograd, Moscow and the industrial areas. The Assembly was dispersed by the Bolsheviks with a shrug—and casuistical explanations of the difference between socialist and bourgeois revolutions. Bolshevik weakness in the country-side was also displayed in the constitution of 1918 when the weighting of urban and rural voters was three or four to one in favour of the former.

The C.P.P. started in the towns and more specifically Accra in the South. It was, unlike the C.P., a nationalist

party and therefore did not have Marxism's strong anti-
pathy to 'rural idiocy'; yet it too was weakest in the
rural areas. This needs no extensive explanation arising
as it did from the hostility of the still powerful rural
chiefs to the thrusting new boys. In the 1951 General
Election there was a variety of voting and electoral
techniques which makes analysis difficult, but the overall
impression is that although by far the largest party the
C.P.P. was strongest in the Municipalities. 'The urban support for nationalism was by far the strongest of any of the
major electoral areas' (Apter, 1955, 201). The C.P.P. obtained
95% of the votes cast in Municipal elections where 47%
of the registered people actually voted. In the rural southern
electoral college the C.P.P. won 29 of the 33 seats and 79%
of the college votes. Finally the elections by the Territorial
councils (mainly dominated by rural chiefs) sent back 19
members few of whom were C.P.P. members.

The urban 'bias' of the C.P.P. was to become clearer
soon after independence, whilst the 'scissors' trend in the
U.S.S.R. simply made evident what had been clear all
along. Both C.P.P. and C.P. were urbanites with a mission
—a vision—of national transformation, and it is clear
that in a peasant-dominated society any transformation
was bound to affect them. Economic and political modernization could only be rapid at the expense of the 'dark
people'.

However, if a pattern of rural-urban division is dis-
cernible in Ghana and Russia, equally significant was the
regional pattern. Both the C.P.P. and the Communist
Party were parties of the most developed areas of their
respective countries, and it soon became apparent that
their hold on the less developed areas was tenuous indeed.
Figures are not available for the earlier period, but in

1922 Russians dominated the party with 72% of total membership (Fainsod, 1953). Russia was an empire composed of diverse nations, tribes, religions and languages held together by the grip of the autocracy; and when the grip was relaxed during the Great War and Civil War many of these countries reverted to narrower local national 'states'. But not only did a series of national revolutions occur, the national branches of the Communist Party were in many cases sympathetic to these nationalist aspirations.

Although within a much narrower geographical framework, the C.P.P. in Ghana faced similar regional problems when it came into power. Ghana, historically, was a geometrical exercise, a series of lines drawn on a map, and was only gradually unified under a single administration, and it was not until 1944 that the Northern Territories were administratively integrated into the rest of the country. Between 1951 and 1957 the country was rocked by a series of particularistic movements in Ashanti and Togo whilst at the same time even more restricted localisms became evident in the Ga Standfast Association in Accra. As in the Russian case members or ex-members of the ruling party were deeply involved in these movements. Neither party was initially disciplined enough to withstand the lures of local national autonomy, whilst the leadership of both parties was deeply committed to centralized politics.

As early as 1903 Lenin had rejected federalism in a multi-national state as economically reactionary and as dividing the proletariat. He appeared, in 1913, to support the right of any nation in Russia to political self-determination—but believed that this right would not be exercised, and also that the right was that of the proletariat *not* of a national bourgeoisie. By December 1917 Stalin openly countered Lenin's view and insisted that 'The principle of self-determination should be a means of fighting for socialism' (Pipes, 1954, 109). In March 1919 Lenin had virtually swung to Stalin's position. Sheer force of circumstances, the revolt of the peripheral nationalities, plus intervention, caused the party to adopt a federal solution as a preliminary to the establishment of socialism and the end of state power. Meanwhile there was a powerful and relatively centralized party!

Unlike Lenin it appears that Nkrumah had not thought, or at least published, on the 'nationality' problem in Ghana before it was presented to him in the form of the National Liberation Movement in Ashanti and the Togo revolt. There are a few hints that he thought in terms of a united West Africa—but nothing about the form it would take. When the federal issue did arise in 1954 he went some way to meeting it by suggesting a measure of limited regional devolution. By this time, however, the Ashanti 'nationalists' were demanding a federal system of government 'To secure due recognition of the economic social and cultural background of the respective regions of the Gold Coast'.

Thus both C.P. and C.P.P. can be understood as movements by technically more advanced groups into less advanced areas. But there was a difference. Prior to the British occupation and control of the Gold Coast the militarily better organized Ashanti were pressing on the coastal peoples and might well have secured control. In the Russian empire on the other hand the encroachment was from the White Russians of 'Muscovy' outwards, and the Bolsheviks simply continued this process. The C.P.P. in fact was a dominantly coastal party which inherited a strong position from the British and utilized this to control Ashanti.

The argument up to this point has been a simple one: it is that the C.P. and the C.P.P. had a great deal in common in terms of organization, of thinking about the rôle of organization, of assessment of the central importance of economic development of the nationalistic or tribal difficulties that faced upon assuming power. I have also suggested other similar problems that faced both parties, i.e. a small unskilled labour force, inadequate standards of health, insufficient educational provision and poor communications. The major instruments of social change—the parties—were mainly urban in rural communities; they were composed of mainly young people having scant experience of political office and both emerged from political situations best described as authoritarian.

These then were some of the features common to both situations. The argument is not that the C.P.P. was a Communist Party, however, but rather that common situations and ideas are likely to engender common responses and policies. In the following chapters I shall examine the immediate response of the C.P. and the C.P.P. to office and responsibility.

2
Prelude to control

When the two parties assumed power their immediate response was moderate, at least in terms of later developments, and very considerable attention was paid to consolidating the basis upon which their power rested. The internal organization of both was tightened up and professionalized, other parties were severely hampered or banned and opposition groups in the country dispersed or limited. Power was also consolidated within the parties by the rapid control exercised over hitherto independent secondary associations such as the trade unions. In retrospect it is possible to see the earlier period as one of political consolidation combined with economic experiment on a piecemeal level.

The reason for the similarity of this control pattern in both countries is not difficult to discern. In neither country was the eventual ruling party really responsible for the 'troubles' preceding their takeover. The preceding revolutions had developed slowly, they were spontaneous and inchoate and given shape, direction and an *organizational* framework by the Communist Party and the Convention Peoples Party. Both parties had to control a revolution before they could start one.

The problem of unification

The most urgent problem facing the new regimes was that of unification in the face of opposition from local interests. At the beginning of 1918 the Tzarist empire collapsed into its constituent parts; Lenin then had either to leave the new 'countries' to develop or re-integrate them by force. He chose the latter, but accepted a type of federal constitution. How this was achieved is not, for our purpose, significant, but what is important are the implications of the re-integration on the Party. In a word, it became militarized in its concept of discipline, 'Every decision must first of all be carried out, and only later can it be appealed to the proper party organ. In this sense the party must possess in the present epoch virtually a military discipline' (Lenin in Pipes, 1954).

Given the necessity of maintaining power this was certainly true since the C.P. was a tiny minority (.00025% of population) (Fainsod, 1953). But it was not sufficient merely to discipline the party, the opposition had to be removed! Thus the internal and external controls proceeded at the same time, between 1917 and 1921. Further, the economically moderate New Economic Policy also played a part in disabusing the Left of the party whilst the clamp on the opposition led them to terrorism and violence.

Intra-party controls

As a minority convinced of its own rectitude, the Bolsheviks showed less than sympathy towards those parties opposing the Bolshevik seizure of the revolution. The Bolsheviks in December 1917 admitted the Left Socialist Revolutionaries into the government—by July 1918 they were out. The break came on the question of grain confiscation, on the use of force against political opponents

19

and finally on the debate about peace with Germany which they opposed (Schapiro, 1955).

Menshevism, after the revolution, was not really of serious political importance. But very different were the Socialist Revolutionaries who enjoyed mass peasant support and won a majority of seats to the Constituent Assembly. However, their support was badly organized and their organization and discipline almost non-existent.

Lack of internal discipline, lack of inter-opposition unity and lack, in many cases, of political realism left the opposition parties fairly easy prey for the Bolsheviks. Precisely the same was true in Ghana where the opposition to Nkrumah displayed an intransigence and propensity to split that was positively Trotskyist. However, legal opposition existed in the U.S.S.R. until 1921 although it was subjected to restrictions that made it impotent; thus in March 1920 the Moscow Mensheviks complained of 'Innumerable acts of violence against the will of the electors, terrorization, pressure, and other abuses, which took place in the electoral campaign'. Despite the campaign against the Mensheviks, at the end of the Civil War amongst the proletariat 'Mensheviks, pro-Mensheviks, and other anti-Communists together far outweighed the Communists and their sympathizers' (Schapiro, 1955, 201). The Communists simply arrested, harried or disbanded unions where their legal opponents were strong; they were banned in 1921.

Within the C.P. a somewhat similar process of manufacturing unity ran parallel with the external trend. Intellectually the party was never as united as is often supposed, and the assumption of power laid the basis for numerous intra-party disputes. These centred upon the question of peace with Germany, factory management and the organization of Bolshevik forces in the

20

Civil War. Roughly, the party split in two: those who favoured partisan formations often favoured worker's control and a continuation of the war, whilst Lenin and Trotsky favoured peace combined with conventional military formations and one-man industrial control.

The 10th Party Congress (1921) clamped internal opposition. Amidst difficulties, surrounded by enemies and saboteurs, it was necessary to cease criticism and, more important, all factions with separate programmes had to cease activity. Free discussion, or at least its organization, was now illegal both within and without the C.P.

Control of opposition

Ghanaian developments in the early period resembled the Russian trend although, of course, the milieu was far less violent and strained; there was no civil war proper in Ghana although developments in Togo and Ashanti showed the possibilities. A significant difference between the two parties, however, must be stressed. If the C.P. showed clear intellectual and emotional strains in 1917–21 there is not much evidence that they were a result of self-seeking; the same cannot be said of most C.P.P. dissidents. By the 1954 election evidence of intra-party stress and regional differences emerged.

In the North the Northern Peoples Party was formed in April 1954 to protect the region against 'carpet-baggers' from the C.P.P. and ensure its 'political and social development' (Austin, 1964, 184). Adopting much of the C.P.P.'s political panache, the N.P.P. was based on chiefs and commoners and its success in the 1954 elections was ominous. In that election, after only a few months of preparation, it and its associates won 15 seats to the C.P.P.'s 8. Equally dangerous was the Ghana Congress Party which was based upon Ashanti and led by intellectuals closely

C

associated with the chiefs together with a number of ex-C.P.P. members. Badly beaten in the 1954 election when it won one seat in Ashanti, it heralded the much more formidable Northern Liberation Movement (N.L.M.).

The N.L.M. was founded in Kumasi in September 1954, soon after the election and no mistake could be made about its appeal which was specifically to Ashanti nationalism and economic grievances. 'Their forbears through toil and sweat, through bitter experience had erected a Nation which was admired and respected by foreigners. It was the duty of the present generation to see that Ashanti was not lost through an unsuitable Constitution for the Gold Coast.' This, a statement of the Asantenene, was the true stuff of nationalism.

And, unlike the Gold Coast as a whole, the Ashanti had a commonly accepted national symbol in the Golden Stool, they had a more or less unified and defined national territory, their language was more or less continuous with the national area and they had a long history of resistance to British incursions.

By most standards they were a nation, a nation faced with the possibility of becoming incorporated into a state which was not yet a nation. Hence, it could not be a matter for surprise that the National Liberation Movement was as successful as it proved to be. Equally, it is hardly surprising that in an all out political war both parties committed excesses, and in an unequal struggle the N.L.M. was bound to be defeated and the C.P.P. to become more intransigent.

The struggle between the parties amounted to a political war between two armed ideas. And there is little doubt that the N.L.M. was a threat to the C.P.P. hegemony and its social regional basis, resembling in some respects the

22

Northern Peoples Congress in Nigeria, was adequate to
support an opposition.

As with the N.P.P. the new party showed its local
strength by winning over many of the C.P.P.'s supporters
(Hodgkin, 1961). Indeed it had its origins in the Asante
Youth Association which in 1949 under Krobo Edusei
had spearheaded the C.P.P. drive into Ashanti. By 1955
no less than 18 of 21 members of the N.L.M. executive
were ex-C.P.P. Politically the most important N.L.M. plank
was federalism, but with the N.P.P. in the North, the
N.L.M. in Ashanti and the C.P.P. firmly based in the
South the suggestion could easily have led to a series of
single party regions on the Nigerian model.

Another localist challenge to the C.P.P. came from the
Togoland Congress in Eastern Ghana. Here, although the
details were complex, the underlying issues were relatively
simple. The leadership of the Togoland Congress saw the
C.P.P. as plotting to undermine Ewe nationalism and in-
corporate the territory into Ghana. Like Ashanti the Ewe
area was cocoa-rich and like Ashanti resented taxes which
subsidized the south. Contesting the 1954 election on the
basis of an unified Ewe homeland the Congress won 3
seats, all in the South, to the C.P.P.'s 8 seats.

In one sense the C.P.P. had done well, it was *the*
nationally organized party, and it had won a majority of
votes and seats in two of the four regions. But it had lost
its grip on Ashanti and the North, only narrowly won in
Trans Volta, whilst 45% of its total vote came from the
South; this after five years in office during which it had
not hesitated to use *all* the advantages of office to increase support. In addition, as with the C.P., intra-party
dissension began soon after assuming office; hitherto active party members had joined opposition groups and
within the party there developed 'left' pressure for the

more radical approach to self-government. In other words, whilst it was *the* most popular party the evidence suggests it was no longer a popular party. This trend was to continue to the end.

Faced with a similar range of problems the C.P.P. acted in a manner comparable to the Bolsheviks. As with the C.P. the Convention experienced a rapid increase in membership soon after taking office—and this increase led to problems of control since it was true of both parties that 'The new recruits who formed the party base were frequently illiterate, sometimes turbulent, badly disciplined and unreliable' (Fainsod, 1953, 69). By August 1952 C.P.P. claimed membership was about 700,000 (14% of the population) and the party executive planned to 'cope with the tremendous growth of the Party in order to ensure a more solid, militant and disciplined organization' (Austin, 1960, 171). A number of prominent left-wing C.P.P. men were expelled and attempts were made to control the regional organization through secretaries appointed and paid from Accra. At the same time the C.P.P. stressed the need for ideological training and with this in mind organized the National Assocation of Socialist Student Organizations in 1954.

By 1955 Nkrumah dominated the party executive as Life Chairman with the right to select a majority on the Central Committee of the Executive. Policy was formulated either by Nkrumah or by the Central Committee, central control was also exercised over elective offices and 'the Life Chairman ultimately selected the candidates' (Bretton, 1956). By 1954 Nkrumah had imposed some discipline on the party; large numbers of local rebels were expelled and the parliamentary left mauled (Apter, 1955).

This much was achieved whilst the country was still technically dependent on the U.K. Such dependence made

24

an all-out offensive against regionalism politically difficult. After independence things went very differently with the opposition.

National integration and control

Independence was granted in March 1957 under an agreed constitution which provided for the establishment of five regional assemblies entrenched with a provision requiring two-thirds assent to change in both regional assemblies and central legislature. Rioting actually broke out in South Togo when the country was engaged in celebrating independence, but this was easily suppressed. Far more significant was the trouble in Accra amongst the Ga people who had been strong C.P.P. supporters. Even before independence members of the Ga community who were in the C.P.P. bitterly complained about the lack of inner-party democracy and alleged favouritism. In July 1957 they formed an organization called the Ga Standfast Association which obtained wide local support and coincided with grievances of the ex-Servicemen and a Motor Drivers Union over housing allocations and the limitation of vehicle licences. Serious disturbances threatened in the very heartland of C.P.P. and amongst social groups hitherto most closely associated with the ruling party. Compare this with the 1921 Kronstadt Revolt! This too broke out where previously loyalty was strong, it was also associated with strikes amongst workers and it too resulted in demands for inner and inter-party democracy.

Government reaction was rapid and draconic. The extra-party opposition was attacked in its regional strongholds by a dual process of under-mining the chiefs and a Bill —the Avoidance of Discrimination Act (December 1957) —which made illegal the continuation or formation of parties founded on religious, tribal or regional basis. This amounted to a ban on all opposition parties as they existed at the time. Even before this the leadership of a religious party, the Moslem Association Party, was deported. Under an Emergency Powers Act of December 1957 and a Preventive Detention Act of July 1958 the government was granted wide powers against opposition, and like Lenin before him Nkrumah was marked for assassination. Thus by the end of 1958 the government had virtually eliminated the legal framework of opposition and began to squeeze it in the regions.

Squeezing the regional strongholds of the opposition meant controlling or replacing the traditional authorities of the country. Nkrumah saw the chiefs as a hindrance to his nationalism and, although he frequently went out of his way to pay lip service to them, his basic proposition was always that chieftaincy 'must in large measure adapt itself to the changing requirement of changing time' (Nkrumah, 1961, 35). In fact almost everything the C.P.P. government did undermined the chiefs' authority. For example, one of the first major legislative achievements of the Nkrumah government was the Local Government Ordinance of 1951 which set up a national system of local government authorities on an elective basis and without a place for chiefs. Three Acts passed during 1959 virtually put the chiefs at C.P.P. disposal since the government was authorized to withdraw recognition, seize stool property and stool revenue. This almost destroyed the social basis of traditional opposition. Thus the opposition was crushed by the party/state machine and *not* by the old C.P.P. techniques of rallies, appeals to national pride or even by splitting the cocoa-farming chiefs and cocoa farmers from the landless labourer.

Similarly in Russia, the Bolsheviks paid lip service to

local traditions 'All you, whose mosques and shrines have been violated . . . Henceforward your beliefs and customs, your national and cultural institutions, are declared free and inviolable' (Wheeler, 1960, 12). But this attitude was short-lived. Even a Marxist form of Islam was denounced and Sultan Galiyeu, its founder, banished from the party (Wheeler, p. 20). In Turkestan the native intelligentsia and leadership, both modern and traditional, was categorized as an exploiting class and allowed very little scope for political activity (Park, 1957). Nationalism in the Ukraine, although existing as a minority intellectual plea prior to 1917, actually flowered into a popular majority movement only after the collapse of the Tsarist government, and the establishment of a German puppet government. There followed a period of internal confusion which so exhausted land and people 'that Bolshevism's patient workers were able to slip into power almost unchallenged' (Adams, 1963). As in the other areas of Bolshevik occupation the new authorities made concessions to local customs, language, etc., but kept control of the sources of political power (Rywkin, 1964).

One other common organizational feature of the first period is worth noting, the virtual incorporation of independent secondary associations into the party or their replacement by a party controlled association. Broadly, the reasons for this *gleich schaltung* were both ideological and practical. Nkrumah's Nationalism and Marxism-Leninism have at least one thing in common, they have wide or total implications for social life, they are all embracing social philosophies. Politics and the political is all, 'Seek ye first the political Kingdom'.

Reinforcing the ideological trend is the origin of the C.P.P., which, like so many African political parties was closely associated with secondary associations; seeking to

27

engage the whole person in the anti-colonial struggle the C.P.P. from the beginning established close links with youth groups, trade unions, ex-servicemen and women's organizations (Wallerstein, 1964). Nkrumah's message was clear and loud, 'Let individuals, men and women, join any of the political organizations, farmers' unions, trade unions, co-operative societies, youth movements . . . No individual person should be without membership in some organization' (Nkrumah, 1961, 15).

Although by no means as deeply engaged in Russian society, the Bolsheviks made up for this by the intensity of their ideological claims to pre-eminence. Marxism was a tool of total philosophical understanding; it was correct and all others were false. As a body orientated towards the working class it was to be expected that the Bolsheviks would have made their major impact—or attempted to do so—upon the organized proletariat, that is the trade unions. For Lenin the problem was to harness the economic struggle of the unions to Bolshevism whilst explaining to the trade unions the political implications of their activity. Trade unionism could never autonomously become a reliable political force, it needed Bolshevik direction.

Weak before the Bolshevik seizure, after it the party had no intention of allowing the unions real authority. In a formula to become familiar in Ghana Tomsky the leading Bolshevik unionist explained that, 'The sectional interests of groups of workers have had to be subordinated to the interests of the entire class'. Given the party claim to a monopoly of political wisdom the implication was clear! Even claims to a share in management was denied the unions, not on ideological grounds but on the basis of practical necessity since efficiency was needed if the civil war was to be successfully concluded.

Within Ghana a similar series of events culminated in a similar relationship. Trade unionism was weak, ephemeral and badly organized: 56 unions in 1949 with about 18,000 members and a T.U.C. lacking both funds and authority. The T.U.C. which was independent of, but in sympathy with, the C.P.P. initiated a strike in support of Nkrumah's 'positive action' campaign of January 1950. The T.U.C. collapsed under the financial strain. With encouragement from the administration the T.U.C. was reformed in 1951 under 'moderate' non-political leaders. In response to this the C.P.P. trade union leaders formed a rival Ghana Trade Union Congress (G.T.U.C.), a creature of the C.P.P. under the leadership of Mr Turkson-Ocran, Nkrumah's personal secretary. This front organization in fact received no real support from the working class.

As in the Russian case, although some unions and leaders were sympathetic to the party, this was not true of all, and as in Russia it was not until the party was firmly in control of political power that it was able to control the unions. (In 1955 two of the biggest unions formed a Congress of Free Trade Unions and affiliated to the N.L.M.; it collapsed with the N.L.M. after the 1956 elections.) However, as in Russia, the party took care to control the 'ultras' of the unions—who had criticized C.P.P. compromise on the issue of immediate self-government in August 1952 and attacked foreign control of the proposed Volta scheme—by expelling the Marxists Anthony Woode, Turkson-Ocran and Pobee Biney. But *anschluss* was effected in Ghana within 18 months of independence through an Industrial Relations Act which set up twenty-four unions, gave the party-controlled Ghana T.U.C. wide powers over the unions and prohibited strikes in the public sector. Introducing the Bill the Minister of Labour struck a note later to become a dominant theme of government-union relations: 'the national character of my government allows for harmony between employers and workers'. By the early 1960's this meant that there could be no dispute between government and workers.

In neither country was this control simply for the sake of control, but rather because the unions were seen as part of a wider more comprehensive social reality. As with the rest of Nkrumah's thinking this wider reality was not confined to Ghana, and the Ghana T.U.C. was to be a part of his wider tactic of Pan-African political influence which was to culminate in a distinctively African style of politics. The T.U.C. thus had an international rôle defined by Nkrumah in October 1959 as establishing an All-African Trade Union Federation 'dedicated to the movement for the independence and unity of Africa'. Later in October the T.U.C. disaffiliated from the Western-dominated International Congress of Free Trade Unions and called a conference to establish an All-African Trade Union Federation. The T.U.C. was simply a part of a wider-ranging political strategy. As Kwame Nkrumah put it in October 1959, 'I would like to emphasize my determination to maintain the unity of the country for our economic, political and social reconstruction. The reorganization of the Farmers Council, the Co-operative movement, the Builders Brigade, the Trade Union Congress ... are all designed to achieve this objective. The C.P.P. is the political vanguard of these movements' (Nkrumah, 1961, 187). Precisely the same was true of Russia: both had to control prior to mobilization! And in both countries the unions were to become simply transmission belts for official government policies, in no way independent and with no recognition that the interests of regime and workers might differ.

The party in Russia was far more urbanized in its

membership than the C.P.P.; indeed, it is possible to regard the Bolsheviks as besieged by peasants until the break-out of collectivization in the late 1920's. Before that the C.P. confined itself to the towns, initially making foraging expeditions (War Communism) into the countryside, in 1922 contenting itself with a moderate taxation policy and from 1928 setting out to urbanize Russia. The same was not true of Ghana except to a limited extent: if it was to be developed rapidly into an industrially based country then (i) farming productivity had to increase, and (ii) real farming income had to increase considerably less rapidly than productivity increases would otherwise have warranted. In both countries the major resources were outside the towns and, hence, the common problem of controlling the rural areas arose.

Initially the Bolsheviks responded not to any ideological imperative but simply to the need for food for the towns; the difficulty was that the towns were producing nothing to tempt grain from peasant barns. Hence, 'People from the towns . . . were sent out *to fetch the grain*' (Maynard, 1962). But they sought to obtain it from a country-side ravaged by war, disease and starvation. The next step, the New Economic Policy, was an interim measure; 'Lenin proposed to retire a little, to retreat for a while nearer the base . . . so as to gather strength and resume the offensive.' It involved regular taxes in kind from the peasants, freedom of enterprise and encouragement of peasant initiative.

Under N.E.P. Russian agriculture gradually recovered, light industry markedly increased, but little capital formation took place, heavy industry lagged, and it was to heavy industry that Lenin looked; 'Unless we save heavy industry, unless we restore it . . . we shall be doomed as an independent country.' But the basic defect was built into the system: the terms of trade between urban and rural favoured the former and gave the peasant little incentive to market surplus produce. Hence under N.E.P., even if things gradually improved, Russia had only a small surplus available for export whilst food shortages curtailed the urban proletariat (Erlich, 1950).

Thus in Russia the agricultural picture in the first period of party rule is one of relatively loose control with minimal impingement on the countryside. 'Beneath the surface of sovietization, the life of the peasant flowed on in its accustomed way relatively untouched by the great political and social overturn which the revolution engendered in the cities (Fainsod, 1958, 141).

Nationalism in the Gold Coast was closely associated with cocoa prices and production, and the cocoa farmers had a standing grievance against European buyers and the British Government (Bourrett, 1960). Returning from London in 1947, Nkrumah was caught up in a maelstrom of troubles amongst which a grievance of the cocoa farmers was prominent: this was the Government's cutting-out campaign. Swollen shoot, a virulent disease of cocoa trees, could then only be combatted by cutting down affected trees and, naturally, farmers disliked this threat to their livelihood. Initially the U.G.C.C. and then, more successfully, the C.C.P. took up the farmers' case, founding in December 1949 a Ghana Farmers Congress; by December 1950 the party was itself sponsoring farmers' candidates (Austin, 1964). In the 1951 election cocoa played an important part with the C.P.P. promising a better deal for the farmers combined with wide ranging social and economic reform. But cocoa was Ghana's major asset, and under C.P.P. administration it increased from 46% of total value exports in 1946 to almost 60% in 1960.

Hence, in its early relations with the farmers the C.P.P. had won a degree of support that eluded the Bolsheviks. But there were two difficulties. Firstly, dependence on an export primary crop left the country dangerously dependent on international terms of trade. Whilst cocoa prices were rising the Government was likely to be able to embark on a reconstruction programme. A more serious short term difficulty concerned the geographical distribution of cocoa production. Something in the region of 50% of total Ghanaian production came from Ashanti (Hill, 1963). A potentially explosive mixture of economic grievance and ethnic particularism was available for the N.L.M., and it was the Government's attempt to stabilize internal cocoa prices that triggered off the Ashanti 'revolt'.

World cocoa prices despite fluctuations gradually rose from 1949 until 1958; in 1954 the Government fixed the price at which its Cocoa Purchasing Company bought from the farmers at 72s. a load. The object was to prevent inflation and to provide the Government with development funds; the move led to serious complaints to the C.P.P.—affiliated United Ghana Farmers Council. A few years later the farmers were again complaining about the government purchase of cocoa. These complaints were justified in many respects since the C.P.C. funds were used, Tammany Hall style, to reward friends, win friends and punish enemies—with the former predominant. The funds constituted a pork barrel of singular flavour, that of cocoa. Culinary defects apart, seen from the cocoa farmers' point of view the portion taken by the C.P.C. benefitted mainly the towns and the politicians leaving the farmer a 'peasant slave'. Up to independence in 1957 the Government gradually alienated the cocoa producers—and it had little alternative since development funds were not available elsewhere. In September 1957 the U.G.F.C. was made the sole farmers' representative body in Ghana, all others being declared illegal.

Thus the rural situations in Ghana and Russia culminated in attempts by the ruling party to extract a development surplus from agriculture. But from the beginning the C.P.P. impact on the countryside was greater than that of the Bolsheviks; Russian agriculture slumbered, to be awoken with a very rude shock in 1927. Such was not the case in Ghana; community development campaigns, Government intervention in crop buying and selling and active persuasion in cocoa improvement culminated in total control by the end of 1957.

Positive control: education

I have up to now concentrated on control similarities between the two countries in the early period; I will now examine the more positive steps taken by the ruling parties. The most important of these was increasing the educational spread. Educational reform was one of the first priorities of both parties; early and massive change was thought imperative. It would not be going too far to describe both the Ghanaian and Soviet revolutions as educational revolutions, with education intimately associated with desired attitudinal changes. Education was to produce New Soviet Man and the African Personality, imbued with love of country and ... work.

Lenin, following Marx, declared in 1917 that administrative tasks 'can easily be performed by every *literate* person' (*The State and Revolution*). He also wished to raise educational standards for economic reasons, suggesting that the *first* 'conditions for raising the productivity of labour is the raising of the educational and cultural level of the masses' (Lenin, 1937, vii, 331). But there was an overall control or public school aspect to

34

education as well. The whole of education and up-bringing shall be directed to their training in communist morals (King, 1963, 3).

In Ghana, as with every other African country, the demand for more education was explosive and it was no coincidence that the C.P.P. Manifestos during pre-independence promised massive expansion of educational facilities. And one of Kwame Nkrumah's major complaints about imperialism was that 'alien rule has not improved education . . . but on the contrary tolerates mass illiteracy' (Nkrumah, 1947, 42). Education also had a social function, 'the training in citizenship which a student can receive here is discipline'. Finally, education was necessary, as Lenin had stressed, to train a cadre of engineers, farmers and administrators (Nkrumah, 1961).

Both Governments initiated far-reaching educational reforms. In Ghana in 1951 an Accelerated Development Plan for Education was issued, probably too quickly, which stressed rapid expansion of primary education. Few curriculum changes were introduced, but emphasis was placed upon children receiving instruction in English from the beginning of their school careers. By 1960 about 41% of Ghanaian children were in primary schools, although regional pattern varied widely from 12% in the North to 60% in Accra. Secondary and technical expansion was less dramatic, by 1960 less than 5% of those entering schools were in secondary education (Foster, 1965, 189). Being a more developed country Russia's on-going educational system was more appropriate for economic development than was that of Ghana which reflected the U.K.'s abysmal failure in technical education.

In February 1918 schools were separated from churches, and in October a two-grade system (8–13 and 13–17) was established. Soviet schools in this period, and especially in urban areas, relaxed discipline, undermined the teachers authority and revised curricula with bewildering rapidity. And it was not until 1926 that the number of children attending schools reached the 1914 total of 10 million. On the other hand, there had been some expansion of technical, professional and university education from about 181,000 in 1914 to about 358,000 by 1927. Thus in contrast to Ghana, Russia concentrated on advanced education, and it was not until the Five Year Plans of the late twenties that really dramatic quantitative educational advance began. Hence, the problem that immediately plagued Ghana—what to do with those 'marginals' who had received only elementary education—did not occur so dramatically in Russia.

Another difference concerned the relatively greater emphasis in Russia on advanced technical education and the curriculum changes in law, social studies and history at the university. The U.S.S.R. was fortunate in inheriting from Tzarist Russia a system which placed some emphasis on technical training. During the 1920's, as in 1914, about 25% of students in further education were in fact in technology, and this does not include agriculture or medicine (Kline, 1957). This was a valuable technical bonus almost totally absent in Ghana until the second development period. Russian higher education was rigidly controlled from the beginning to produce politically conscious soviet citizens. Such was not true of Ghanaian students who tended to favour the opposition.

In fact the Ghanaian university education was closely patterned upon the Oxbridge system of small colleges, high cost, concentration on the Liberal Arts and small numbers of highly qualified students. No thought was devoted to the proposition that a radically different emphasis was needed in an underdeveloped country where

36

divorce between the educated and uneducated is serious enough without the added burden of excessive expenditure on relative inessentials. On the whole the graduates despised agricultural or dirty work and sought a desk; what was needed was far greater emphasis upon middle-level crash agricultural and technical education on the cheap! Not until 1961 was a Ghanaian university devoted to Science and Technology.

In both countries, alongside the developments in education went a stress on ideological training both inside and outside the party. Intra-party ideological training was a response to the danger apparent from the flood of new members and the change from opposition to responsibility. Russian intra-party ideological training was rapidly put onto a regular and extensive basis in order to train reliable administrators from those who entered the party after 1920. A system of party universities was established 'without consideration for the material conditions, lack of teaching staff, high costs etc.' and by 'the early 1920's a differentiated system of institutions for idealogical and political education was in operation'. By 1927 some 5,000 institutions were attended by 245,000 students and by 1930 attendance at party schools was claimed to be one million (Katz, 1956). These 'intellectual' efforts far exceeded those of the C.P.P. which did not have an ideological 'university' until the early 1960's.

National ideology in Ghana

Initially the C.P.P. was simply a radical nationalist party without a coherent political philosophy of any sort beyond opposition to an undefined imperialism, colonialism, racialism, tribalism and all forms of national and racial oppression. In addition the party claimed itself as socialist and, operationally more important, favoured 'the demand

37

for a West African Federation and ... Pan-Africanism'. But it was not until the mid-1950's that these slogans were underpinned with a relatively coherent intellectual basis; only the commitment to the wider African unity was pursued from the beginning. Thus the Five Year Plan introduced in 1952 proposed an expenditure of £120 m. of which social services would take up about 33% and an ambitious scheme of road and rail communication developed. It was essentially an attempt to modernize the economic infra-structure of the country to which almost 89% of the proposed investment was devoted. This allocation had nothing to do with socialist theory, it was a recognition of necessity (Birmingham, Neustadt and Omaboe, 1966, i).

Precisely the same was true of the Government's attitude to private and foreign investment; resources were not available internally hence: 'it was my Government's earnest wish that those with capital to invest would seek the opportunity which existed in the Gold Coast' (Nkrumah, 1959, 129). And Ghanaian incentives to foreign investment were attractive, but little was attracted in and indeed, there was a net loss of private capital between 1957 and 1961 and very little was attracted to import substitutes. What private investment there was went into mining and commercial infra-structure to the neglect of manufacturing—except brewing!

Insofar as there was an ideology then it was one of social and psychological reconstruction and it was to these that Nkrumah devoted a considerable amount of attention. Like the Soviets, Nkrumah was aware that failure in Ghana would be far reaching since the hopes of 'millions of Africans living in our great continent are pinned upon the success of our experiment here' (Nkrumah, 1961, 60).

Essentially the psychological reconstruction consisted of two elements (i) the struggle against corruption and a sense of inferiority and (ii) the production of proof that Africans could govern themselves and prosper economically. Nkrumah stressed the dangers of corruption as early as 1951 claiming that 'Bribery and corruption, both moral and factual, have eaten into the whole fabric of our society and they must be stamped out if we are to achieve any progress'. Ghanaian society had been corrupted by colonialism and would be attacked by imperialism in various disguises (these were later erected into a curiously eclectic hagiography). But whispers of corruption on a wide scale were widespread—and true. Ghana was governed by new and inexperienced men, old standards were gradually eroding but bureaucratic norms were not widespread and the pace of economic development was rapid; an almost ideal broth within which corruption could flourish. 'Socialism,' remarked the golden-bedded Krobo Edusei, 'doesn't mean that if you've made a lot of money, you can't keep it.' It certainly didn't.

The fight against corruption was to be of little avail. The corruptors were themselves high priests of anticorruption. Possibly more successful was that against what Fanon called 'the colonization of the personality' and Mannoni 'the dependence complex'. That is, an important element in the early stage of the Ghanaian revolution was the freeing of African negroes and the formation of 'the African Personality'. This crusade had two aspects, (i) an insistence on the value of Africa's traditional heritage, and (ii) an analysis of Africa's rôle in the modern world. Sometimes the former took bizarre forms such as Africans teaching Egyptians medicine etc. on murals, but the intention was clear.

Closely connected with the rediscovery and re-

39

emphasizing of negro humanity and history was the insistence on Africa's rôle in the world, on its contribution to global politics. This involved non-alignment and neutralism; neither were interpreted as negative policies, but as positive responses to the Cold War to ameliorate it in Europe and keep it out of Africa. In all of this Nkrumah kept rather more than a weather eye cocked towards the rest of Africa. He saw Ghana as a beacon, a guiding light to dependent Africa and an example to be followed. 'It was to be hoped that our efforts would bring a ray of hope of a brighter future not only to our own people, but to all in other parts of Africa *who looked to us for inspiration in their struggles to be free*' (Nkrumah, 1961, 153).

Nkrumah, like Lenin, was also interested in bringing about amongst Ghanaians attitudinal changes towards ideas believed to be functionally appropriate in an industrializing society. The extended family, for instance, was thought of as discouraging individual initiative and thrift and some direct steps, like the building of small unit housing in the Volta, were taken to encourage the nuclear family. Again, nepotism, polygamy, religious festivals and expensive weddings and funerals were specifically mentioned by him as obstacles to economic progress (Nkrumah, 1963). Like his Russian brother before him, the Ghanaian worker, if Nkrumah got his way, was due for a painful lesson in applied psychology *à la mode* Weber.

Marxism in Russia

Bolshevik ideology was, of course, far more intellectually cohesive than was nationalism, but this was hardly to its advantage in terms of actually ruling and maintaining power in Russia, since Marx had hardly discussed the mechanics of socialist rule, and Lenin's own thoughts before the revolution were hardly more adequate. The actual form of Communist domination—via the Soviets—was accidental and 'The Bolsheviks had never proclaimed the one-party state as their avowed policy before the revolution' (Schapiro, 1955, 354). N.E.P. was simply a 'retreat' forced upon the party by circumstances as—given the decision to go it alone—was almost everything else. For example, the 1918 constitution 'did not so much create new forms of government as register and regularize those which were in course of being established by unco-ordinated initiative in the aftermath of the revolutionary upheaval' (Carr, 1950, vol. 1, 124). Such examples could be multiplied almost indefinitely, but the point is a simple one: the party had to use what was available and learn, as Lenin put it, 'from ordinary salesmen . . . (who) have had ten years warehouse experience and know the business' (Fainsod, 1953, 99). The Bolsheviks had an ideology but the immediate political priorities were determined by circumstances.

Lenin believed that the *immediate* task of the Bolsheviks was to 'retain state power' and to achieve this two things were necessary, (i) to take advantage of imperial rivalry and (ii) 'instil in the oppressed and labouring masses confidence in their own power'. The Bolshevik seizure of power was based on the weakest link proposition, that when bourgeois power was broken in Russia, where it was weakest, the revolutionary example would spread. 'Proletarians of all countries are realizing more and more clearly every day that Bolshevism has indicated the right road . . . that Bolshevism *can serve as a model tactic for all*' (Lenin, 1937, vii, 183). Bolshevism in Russia, as with nationalism in Ghana, was thus an example and a crusade.

In foreign affairs both leaders understood their revolutions as the beginning of a process, as the nucleus of a wider revolt: 'we shall be able to render serious assistance to the socialist revolution in the West ... only to the extent that we are able to fulfil the organizational task that confronts us' (Lenin, 1937, 314). Nkrumah was less forthcoming on actual assistance, arguing that 'We feel confident in being able to inspire our fellow Africans still under foreign domination to achieve their freedom by ourselves making a success of our freedom' (Nkrumah, 1961, 152). Both countries were surrounded by enemies determined to undermine the fragile unity of the new regimes 'not merely by military means, but by economic penetration, cultural assimilation, ideological domination, psychological infiltration, and subversive activities' (*ibid.*, 128). And Lenin warned the Bolsheviks of imperialist states bordering on Russia, controlled by 'capitalists who hate socialism and are eager for plunder', which might invade at any time (Lenin, 1937, 313). Hence in both countries, from the beginning, eternal vigilance was imperatively necessary—and was to become more and more the price of dictatorship.

Corruption in Ghana and the U.S.S.R.

If the new states were to inspire Africans and proletarians of other countries it was necessary to inspire Ghanaians and Russians with a sense of mission. This was a function of the party. But what if the party was corrupt or became corrupted? In 1921–22 the Communist Party was purged of 140,000 members who were 'rascals, bureaucrats, dishonest or wavering Communists'; 34% were expelled for 'passivity', 25% for crimes such as bourgeois way of life, drunkeness and careerism, and a further 9% for bribe-taking. This was by no means the end of the trouble, and up to the 1927 purge about 1% of members were expelled for 'drunkenness, careerism or dishonesty (which) remained a feature of party life' (Schapiro, 1960, 232). Maynard, indeed, writes of N.E.P. as a 'saturnalia of corruption, gambling and prostitution' with 'the Soviet authorities ... horrified at the corruption which they found among the heads of state trusts and party members' (Maynard, 1962, 194).

This was a 'tomorrow we may die' type of corruption, probably engendered from within the ranks of N.E.P. men harried by regulations and regarded as products of the historical rubbish-bin, but able to bribe—and situationally open to extortion. It was also, as in Ghana, practised upon and within a new political class, but unlike Ghana in its cruder form it was vigorously attacked.

Yet after all is said it remains true that leadership of the Bolsheviks was, on the whole, not corrupt in anything like the way that the leadership of the C.P.P. was. This was probably a consequence of the long years spent in the atmosphere of the underground where the waverer or the opportunist soon fell by the wayside. It is also likely that the personal near-asceticism of Lenin combined with a strong anti-bourgeois, anti-property element in Marx and Marxism combined to combat the more blatant forms of corruption.

Thus it was in the context of widespread bribery etc. —oiling or gritting the wheels is unimportant—that the U.S.S.R., like Ghana, attempted to 'instil in the oppressed and labouring masses confidence in their own power' Up to the late 1920's in the U.S.S.R. this effectively meant the urban proletariat, since penetration into the rural areas was minimal, and the process involved disciplining workers new to industrialism and closely connected with rural life. Lenin, commenting on the Immediate Tasks of Soviet Government insisted that 'The Russian worker

43

is a bad worker compared with the workers of advanced countries' and demanded the introduction of better discipline and work control (Lenin, 1937, 332). Discipline was to be introduced through a system of card indexes on productivity and bonus schemes, but they came to nothing since the administrative framework was lacking. More important, the money economy was collapsing and workers were taking about 50% of what they produced for direct barter. Again, the towns were diminishing in size and industrial workers were reverting to the land (Deutscher, 1950). Thus the proletariat was dissolving into peasantry and petty traders!

N.E.P. was the response to this; it involved increased control over the unions combined with a 'liberalization' of labour policy. For example, direction of labour ceased in 1922—it was not necessary with a growing unemployment problem. However, economically N.E.P. was a success, at least in terms of utilizing existing industrial and agricultural capacity which by 1928 was 110% based on 1913. Politically N.E.P. represented a breathing space for Bolshevism during which control over Russian life and institutions was gradually increased and the party disciplined, but in everyday life the regime remained detached. Ideological penetration of the rural masses was attempted but with scant success—in 1928 less than 4% of agricultural production was co-operative. Further, the number of peasant farms in Russia had actually increased since 1917 by some 8 millions to 25 millions, whilst only one-third of the grain sold to the towns in 1914 was then being sent. Russia in the 1920's was more a peasant society than in 1914. Greater agricultural production for the urban market was essential. In the towns further efforts at control were made, but even there emphasis was more on Taylorism than on Marxism. The Soviet

44

élite concentrated on strengthening its hold on the unions, on heavy industry, the towns and the armed forces, and on secondary and technical education. But most important of all was the party.

In the mid-1920's the Communist Party was in process of coming under the control of Stalin's Secretariat. Debate within the party was still wide-ranging, but it was debate without a power basis—at least as far as the Zinoviev-Kamenev Leningrad faction was concerned. This was evident at the 14th Party Congress in December 1925 when practically the whole of the conference delegates were chosen through Stalin's apparatus. Opposition had been rendered harmless and the party united and disciplined. The Soviet road to industrialization and its attendant miseries was well prepared.

Not so in Ghana. The country started off from a lower base, and although prospering it was not as economically developed as Russia in 1917. The educational priorities of the Government were probably wrong in terms of rapid economic development since too much was spent on primary and too little on technical and secondary education. By 1961–62 the party had some semblance of unity, but factionalism was still rife. The unions were apparently well controlled and youth organizations were party-dominated. And the country was still dependent upon a single export crop whose international price was falling rapidly. A great deal had been achieved; increases in cocoa production, plantation crops like rubber, bananas and citrus fruits developed well, internal communications were better, water, plant, hospitals and schools had made astonishing progress. But the country was running down its reserves, and the first Seven Year Plan was to put a massive strain on the economy and the people.

3
The politics of control

Whether or not the phrase 'initial moderation' is a suitable epitaph for the first period is open to doubt, but that the second period in both the U.S.S.R. and Ghana was not moderate is hardly open to question. In the first period both regimes attempted to knit together disparate areas and weld the ruling parties into obedient instruments of rule whilst laying the foundations of a modernized economy and bureaucracy. The first period in both countries saw an end of the old regimes, the bringing of the country under élite domination and the hastening of the educational revolution. The social structure of both countries was relatively untouched and although the political élite had changed, broadly speaking in Russia the abolition of large-scale capitalism was immediately of marginal significance whilst in Ghana the economic basis remained where it always had been, that is foreign-owned or with cocoa farmers.

Increased exploitation

Essentially the second period in both countries was one of increased exploitation combined with further social control. During the earlier period in Ghana both government and private capital investment increased without any decrease in private consumption resources needed to

46

provide for increased capitalization and the expansion of governmental activities did not come from a progressive reduction of internal uses but mainly from abroad' (Birmingham, 1960, *et. al.*, 1960, 44). The high level of private consumption was financed by cocoa exports and the large sterling reserve; but world cocoa prices began to drop in 1958–59 and London reserves also began to drop rapidly. The 1961 Budget introduced higher taxes, more import duties together with a compulsory levy of 5% on wages and 10% on farm incomes. The object was to stem the pressure on imports. By 1962 the internal economy of Ghana was under strain, and it was then that the Seven Year Plan was announced. But it should be stressed that 1951–62 was not a success, at least in terms of building up a manufacturing base although infra-structural progress had been rapid.

In Russia N.E.P. had brought relief from the almost unbearable strains of War Communism, but at the 'expense' of creating an economy dominated by N.E.P. traders and the peasants. Within the party a debate on this problem developed, but even in 1924 conference backing by the secretariat ensured official victory (Carr, 1954, 129). The debate concerned financing industrial expansion, Stalin arguing for moderate price control and financial reform whilst the opposition wished to industrialize by exploiting the peasantry. 'The task of the socialist state' argued Preobrazhensky, the opposition economist, 'consists not in taking from the petty bourgeois producers less than was taken by capitalism, but to take more' (Carr, 1958, 203). This expropriation he wished to be on a prices and tax basis, thus the industrial revolution was to be financed on the basis of 'primitive socialist accumulation'. Stalin later did much the same thing on the basis of collectivization and low agricultural prices.

47

Industrialism and priorities

However, it is important to notice two things. Firstly, as in Ghana, it was not a debate about *whether* to industrialize but *how* and at what pace. Unlike Ghana the most striking increases in production during the first period were achieved merely by putting hitherto idle resources to work again—to re-unite men and machines. In Ghana vast resources were devoted to housing, social infrastructure and business premises. In addition consumer preferences dominated the pattern of imports: 'suits from Switzerland, canned fruits from South Africa, frozen fish from England, gramophone records from the U.S.A.', all were readily available in 1960 (Warner, 1961, 11). The consequence of this was that Ghana had a balance of payments deficit of £53 m., about 10% of available national product. Ghana was still a democracy, at least in terms of economic priorities, at a time when the cost of democracy was high, whilst Russia's economic democracy (up to 1925) merely involved using existing internal resources. Market and widely acceptable priorities had very different implications for the two countries.

But, as in Ghana, the overall balance of the economy was decided by the market rather than by government decision and planning. The picture is one of steadily rising urban and rural standards without any major concentration on basic industry. On the contrary, the 'credit system based on market conditions favoured the consumer industries which yielded quick profits' (Carr, 1958, 331). Thus both countries in the first period actually permitted gradual improvements in living standards. However, in Russia by 1925 it was clear that further expansion necessitated considerable capital investment to produce new capital goods and replace machinery. And at the same time peasant incomes were rising and producing a 'goods famine', that is, a vacuum which could only be filled by importing goods or by producing or by choking off peasant demand. By the 14th Party Congress in 1926 the fundamental decisions had been taken: heavy industry was to be expanded greatly on the basis of internal resources. And it was clear that the major resource was the peasantry.

From 1924 in Russia pressure upon industrial workers to increase productivity—without receiving higher wages —was strong and unremitting; the pressure led to a wave of strikes in 1925 which were followed by wage increases. But in general for a couple of years prior to the advent of the Five Year Plans government resistance to wage increases was stubborn. This was similar to the Ghanaian situation. There, both consumption and public and private investment increased rapidly after independence. An early attempt to squeeze a development surplus —for the Second Five Year Plan—occurred in March 1959 when a voluntary-compulsory reduction in cocoa prices to farmers was announced by Nkrumah. This plan, of £350 million as contrasted with the previous one of £85 million, was to be financed by large external loans, by foreign private investment and from internal taxes. In introducing the plan he stressed, 'It will mean sacrifices and a very considerable increase in the amount of effort'. Nkrumah was right! The plan was an enormously ambitious one and almost certain to cause inflation unless draconic taxing was introduced. Its impact can be gauged from the fact that not less than £130 million was for immediate implementation, with about £33 million spent on communications and trade. By 1964 government

49

recurrent expenditure was to reach £60 million in contrast to £47 million in 1958.

In the budget of July 1961 a wider attempt was made to stop the rise in consumption by levying wages and introducing new taxes. The result was price rises and a wave of strikes—illegal under the 1958 Industrial Relations Act—and considerable violence. Thus, in both countries the period just prior to the forced industrialization was one of attempted clamp on living standards which had hitherto risen.

Implications of industrialism

But it was at this point that a significant difference emerges between the Russian and Ghanaian patterns: Russia began to turn inwards and Ghana more resolutely than ever outwards. In Russia the thesis of Socialism in One Country, and in Ghana a massive stress on Pan-Africanism, accompanied the new policy of rapid industrialization. The immediate origins of the doctrine of Socialism in One Country was the struggle within the Party against Trotsky. It was also an attempt by Stalin to step into the ideological shoes of the recently canonized Lenin. But most of all it was simply an adjustment to the *facts* of the European situation which was one of defeat for the revolution wherever it had occurred. The background to the Five Year Plan in 1928 is patently clear: 'the Soviet Government turned its back even more resolutely than before on actual revolutionary activities abroad, (and) retired into semi-isolation' (Kennan, 1960, 77).

The policy was one of withdrawal from foreign adventures combined with a rhetoric of Socialist intransigence. But it was also Russia's declaration of independence and of faith in the capacities and abilities of her enormous population. A declaration of independence from Europe, but also from the peasant who had economically dominated the N.E.P. period.

Nkrumah and foreign affairs

This factor is all-important. Russia constituted a potentially autarchical market needing very little from outside and with a consumer bulk sufficient to maintain an industrial basis of enormous size and complexity. It had repudiated most of its external debt, its industry and banks were home controlled and hence its new industries had not to face fierce competition from foreign concerns. In Ghana all banks and most trade were foreign controlled, in addition, the country was too small to support a modern industrial base. Ghana, if it was to industrialize, had to look beyond its borders. Nkrumah took a stand that in some respects resembled that of the defeated Trotsky. For him the independence of Ghana was simply a beginning, and, therefore, at the Accra Conference in April 1958 and his subsequent tour of Africa, Nkrumah emphasized that 'Ghana's freedom would be meaningless unless linked with the total liberation of the entire continent of Africa'. It soon became clear that Nkrumah was committed to this in more than words, and that for him a corollary was a political union of independent states. Thus in May 1959 he signed a union with Sekou Toure's Guinea which was designed to be the forerunner of a wider political union, and which made a unique provision for the eventual surrender of sovereignty to a wider union. When in July 1961 Mali joined the Union of African States, far-reaching but unimplemented plans for political, economic, military and cultural liaison were drawn up.

However, as early as the 1960 Conference of African

States it was evident that Nkrumah's bid for African leadership and political union was not unchallenged, and in a very hostile speech the Nigerian delegate warned against 'a Messiah who has got a mission to lead Africa'. But as Nkrumah understood the situation, Africa was in danger of 'balkanization', that is, the creation of small client states by the previous occupying powers. Hence, 'When an African balkanized state concludes a pact with its colonial power, then that state has lost control over its foreign policy and is therefore not free'. For Nkrumah the lesson was clear: freedom could be obtained only by a 'political union that will ensure uniformity in our foreign policy'. Anything less, for example a loose economic co-operation, 'means a screen behind which detractors, imperialist and colonialist protagonists and African puppet leaders hide to weaken the concept of any effort to realize African unity and independence'. It is difficult to believe that the élites of the Central African Republic, Chad, French Congo, Dahomey, Gabon, Ivory Coast, Niger, Sierra Leone, and Togoland—all of which he mentioned—can have found much in favour of his concept of political union.

The result of the general failure of independent Africa to follow Nkrumah's lead was predictable. Africa began to be populated by a spectacular variety of colonialist puppets. By 1961 Africa was split into two broad groupings: the Casablanca Group, within which Ghana was in some ways the leaders, and the Monrovia States, far larger than the Casablanca States, less radical, strongly opposed to any idea of political union, and deeply suspicious of Ghanaian pretensions to lead. As President Tubman of Liberia put it in his address to the first Monrovia conference, 'The idea of *Primus inter pares*, first among equals, is destructive of African Unity and Peace ... It will require more than development and larger territory to assume leadership of Africa' (Legum, 1962, 53). The speech and the conference were an obvious snub to Nkrumah, and the Ghanaian press launched a barrage of abuse implying that it was all an imperialist plot. When in November 1961 a statue of Nkrumah was bombed he was very quick to see the hand of 'foreign detractors against whom we shall take appropriate action'.

Thus Ghana's second revolution was accompanied by a massive emphasis on foreign politics whilst Russia's was to take place during an officially proclaimed period of peaceful co-existence between Russia and the West. The underlying reasons for this difference have been touched upon, but even here there was a similarity. Both countries felt themselves to be surrounded by a variety of sinister plotters each itching to bring down the socialist regime, preferably by foul means.

Ghana's second 'revolution'

On 1 May 1961 Nkrumah announced that Ghana's political revolution had succeeded and that it was to be followed by the second revolution which consisted of the economic development of Ghana and the total emancipation of Africa. Before examining the economic development proposed and the techniques employed, it is necessary to look again at the political revolution. As we have seen, strenuous attempts had been made to control party and society, yet at a 10th Anniversary rally of the founding of the C.P.P., Nkrumah had to admit, 'the composition of the Party has become socially quite heterogeneous and there is a danger that our socialist objectives may become clouded by opportunistic accommodations and adjustments to *petit bourgeois* elements in our ranks' (1961, 163). What Nkrumah failed to mention is that

E   53 such heterogeneity in party composition is typical of nationalist parties where the independence struggle normally is intense enough to cover up immediate self-interest. He took the opportunity to stress again the need for obedience to party decisions, 'For the strength of our Party depends upon its discipline'. All echelons of the party needed an ideological retread and this was to be undertaken by a section of the party, the Vanguard Activists, and courses of study in socialism were to be undertaken by the parliamentary wing of the party.

Two years later, in April 1961, Nkrumah addressed the nation in a dawn broadcast and deluged the party with criticisms. The party, he complained, spoke with many voices, rumours of bribery and corruption were everywhere, the party was involved in recriminations with the unions and high living was rampant. To counteract all this Nkrumah abolished the separate membership cards of various party affiliates and limited ambassadors' and officials' expenses! (But since, as the Apaloo Report of 1967 pointed out, Nkrumah himself was deeply implicated in the graft and corruption, the authority of his broadcast and subsequent action was vitiated.) Almost everyone in a position of responsibility in the party was more or less involved in the process from Nkrumah down to the local secretary. Also in 1961 Nkrumah opened the Kwame Nkrumah Ideological Centre in Winneba whose rôle was to train party cadres in socialism and party organization; when opening the Institute, Nkrumah reflected that for 'twelve long years . . . no consistent effort has been made to provide party members with the requisite education in the Party's ideology of socialism'. In October 1961 a major change in the rôle of the C.P.P. was announced when the Central Committee ordered the formation of party cells in all indus-

trial and mercantile establishments, farms and government departments. Thus the party which was not united
was to control the country. Standing on the threshold
of the second, the economic revolution, the party was not
an ideologically united body—and it did not become so.
. The 1959–60 re-organization of the C.P.P. had stressed
the rôle of the auxiliary functional organizations, the
T.U.C. and the Ghana Farmers Council, by giving them
special representation on the national executive. With
the decline of the organized political opposition the local
branches tended to become a haven for ex-opposition
people. External opposition to the C.P.P. really became
almost impossible following the discovery of a plot in
1959 to assassinate Nkrumah in which an army officer
and prominent opposition leaders were implicated. By
1961 charges of corruption had been substantiated in
Nkrumah's Dawn Broadcast and in consequence, 'Intrigue,
sycophancy, and mistrust at the centre, and cynicism in
the rural areas, became common' (Coleman and Rosberg,
1964, 301). Effective opposition or a political career were
impossible outside the party; opposition could only come
from within.

Further control in Ghana: the army and the civil service

Alongside the attempted disciplining of the party went
the deification of Nkrumah which was not simply a
matter of statues, picture post cards, portraits and the
paraphernalia of 'charisma', not even claims like 'When
our history is recorded the man Kwame Nkrumah will
be written of as the liberator, the Messiah, the Christ of
our day, whose great love for mankind wrought changes
in Ghana, in Africa, and in the world at large' (*The Party*,
Accra). Nkrumah was very soon to become the un-
challengeable authority in all matters, the ultimate re-

pository of African wisdom. Anticipating this deification and symbolizing the rise of Nkrumaism to a philosophy of history and society was the further encroachment during 1961–2 of the C.P.P. into hitherto independent areas of Ghanaian society. Both army and civil service, which prior to 1961 were relatively free of party influence, were subjected to interference and dogma. Ghana's army and civil service were, from the C.P.P. assumption of office, rapidly Africanized and from 1960 the army was swiftly expanded. Up to about 1960 the army was quite free from 'politics'. Political intervention probably stemmed from inner-party pressure for rapid Africanization and from Nkrumah's desire to set up an African High Command and 'his partners in this concept had made it clear to him that the presence of imperialist officers in Accra was a serious handicap to this ambition' (Alexander, 1965, 95). In September 1961 President Nkrumah dismissed General Alexander, appointed a Ghanaian, Brigadier Otu, to be Army Chief of Staff and assumed the title of Supreme Commander. This was a curtain raiser for things to come. In December 1961 it was reported that the party was considering the establishment of an Army Bureau with the task of 'exchanging ideas of mutual interest on world and local issues' with officers and ordinary ranks.

This can hardly be a matter of real surprise; in its origins, training style and 'ideology' the army was likely to be suffused with British Army values. Such values came into collision with those of the new élite and this was especially true of army professional standards. And the army was also worried by the rumours, current in the middle of 1961, that Nkrumah was contemplating closer military liaison and training with the Soviet Army.

Much the same was true of the Civil Service. Here the

C.P.P. set about politicizing and controlling rather earlier than was the case with the army. A campaign against the Service culminated in Nkrumah's declaration that 'It is our intention to tighten up the regulations and to wipe out disloyal elements in the Civil Service'. There is no evidence that the Service was disloyal to the regime, but it was certainly aloof from the C.P.P., a proletarian and *petit bourgeois* party, and in this it was following the traditions of the British Civil Service. And, as in the army, the expense of training for the Service ensured that senior servants 'were not likely to be regarded as *prima facie* sympathetic to a lower-class political movement' (Tiger, 1962). The party demanded an ending of the services tradition of loyalty to State and insisted upon loyalty to the C.P.P. In the Civil Service the event comparable with the dismissal of Alexander was that in April 1959, of Robert Gardiner, the British trained Ghanaian who headed the key Establishment job. The next step was the setting up of a College of Administration in June 1960 which was to train loyal C.P.P.-oriented civil servants. Very soon after Nkrumah assumed complete control of the Service under provisions of the Republican constitution.

'Socialism' in Ghana

In 1961 was introduced into Ghana the socialist philosophy of Nkrumaism, 'a non-atheistic socialist philosophy which seeks to apply the correct socialist ideas to the solution of our problems'. Intellectually it was based upon the dubious proposition that African society was communalistic and that therefore socialism suited the African temperament. But this farrago apart it had potentially important structural implications for the country's economy.

57

Socialism, the 1962 programme announced, 'can be achieved only by a rapid change in the socio-economic structure of the country ... it is absolutely necessary to have strong ... and highly-centralized government. This means that power must be concentrated in the country's leadership'. In fact by 1962 very considerable power indeed was concentrated in the President's Office which controlled almost every aspect of economic planning, general policy and foreign policy, together with control of the armed forces and the Civil Service. The ministries were evidently in decay as the bewildering rapidity of promotion and demotion and re-organization of ministries suggests. Every section of the people, intelligentsia, workers, farmers and peasants had to pull together. Private enterprise was permitted, indeed encouraged, but primary emphasis was upon State and co-operative undertakings. Also an important object of the party programme, upon which was based the Seven Year Plan, was 'to free our economy from alien control and domination'. Although eventual improvements in living standards were promised the implications of socialism were clear enough : 'in the interests of that socialist objective it will be necessary for all of us (sic) to forgo some immediate personal desire for a greater benefit a bit later on' (Nkrumah, 1963, 123).

A paradox of radicalism

All of this implies a total attack on all problems, a total mobilization of resources. Inspired by Nkrumaist idealism the 'whole nation from the President downwards will form one regiment of disciplined citizens' (Austin, 1964, 409). This programme represents an almost perfect realization of the model of 'Economic Nationalism in Developing States' worked out by H. Johnson (H. Johnson, 1965).

It involved the transfer of real resources to the national élite, the attempt to compensate for this with nationalist and socialist symbols—'psychic gratification'—and growing emphasis on the rôle of the State. The effect of this is to produce a larger middle-class to man the new industry, the growing state bureaucracy and the armed forces: 'nationalism reinforces the trend of modern society towards the establishment of a class structure based on educational attainment'.

This pattern is established almost as soon as the nationalist party takes over, and in Ghana was quite unmistakeable from the beginning of the regime. But in Ghana there was the difficulty that the C.P.P. was not a vehicle of the traditional or the newer élite. The C.P.P. was the party of the verandah boy, the semi-educated standard VI boy and the petty trader. In office all the evidence suggests that it was suspicious of the state bureaucracy and the independent intelligentsia. Yet its programme was sure to produce those who were furthest away from it politically. And it is just this that constitutes the major dilemma for a radical nationalist party. In order to be radical it produces its own enemies! This brings it immediately up against the problem not simply of controlling the traditional élite—when the traditional élite are *not* the nationalist party—but of controlling the new groups without whom the plans and aspirations of the nationalists cannot even get to the paper stage. The greater the rate of development, the more there is the need for control of those produced by the change—and at the very least this needs an effective and disciplined political party.

But it also needs a middle-class élite prepared to forego the life-style of the previous colonialists. In Ghana it is fair to point out that Civil Service salaries and perquisites of office were above that which a poor country can afford and were based on those of the expatriates. It is difficult to know to what extent, but doubtless this accounted in part for the growing imports of high cost foods, spirits and consumer goods, the casino for those earning £1,500 a year and many other anomalies.

Thus it was in Ghana that, as the educational, political and economic changes began to produce results, so the more intense became the attempts to weld the C.P.P. into a controlled instrument of social control.

In the 1960 plebiscite on a new republican constitution and a President for the new state, the C.P.P. by virtue of somewhat dubious electoral methods won about 90% of the total vote with the opposition presidential candidate obtaining 10%. Just prior to the election, lest anyone was under any misapprehension, John Tettegah, an ex-T.U.C. General Secretary, warned electors, 'we shall analyse the votes ward by ward ... and we can take the necessary action against traitors to our cause'. From then on the opposition was in total disarray. The opposition to Nkrumah then began *inside* the party. In May 1961 Nkrumah became Life Chairman of the party and demoted Gbedemah, a 'moderate' founder member.

In an address to the 11th Party Congress in July 1962 Nkrumah spelled out quite clearly the pattern of things to come. The party had to remain above suspicion: 'to achieve this we have periodically to examine ourselves critically ... In future we shall be even more critical of our conduct and actions'. More changes followed in September 1962 when a number of prominent members were purged and others disgraced for owning too much property. This was a direct attack on the 'old Bolsheviks' of the party. At the same time the party completed a reorganization. The change of membership cards was completed, the organization of the party in the regions was strengthened and by July 1962 the C.P.P. was employing 200 full-time officials. And a new enemy was added to the party's rapidly developing list, the 'Budget politician' who complained of taxes and high prices and caused alarm amongst the population. Against the budget politician, the corrupt party official and the disguised imperialist it 'is our duty to exert eternal vigilance'. The next few years were to see eternal vigilance indeed.

Stalin's C.P.

In May 1928 Stalin announced the Five Year Plan, a 130% increase in industrial production on the basis of a surplus to be wrung from a collectivized peasantry (Schapiro, 1960, 364). The proposals were resisted by a 'rightist' group on the Central Committee of the party headed by Bukharin who wished for a more gradual approach, and for a moderate rate of agricultural expropriation. But it was here that a most significant difference between the C.P.P. and the Communist Party in Russia emerges: the Communists observed a party discipline alien to the C.P.P. This had been obvious during the prolonged campaign—just successfully completed—against Trotsky who had not appealed outside the party for support and who, indeed, subscribed with the best to the idea 'my party right or wrong'. (It is difficult to imagine a C.P.P. activist believing, as Trotsky certainly did, that 'One can be right only with the party and through the party, for history has created no other road for the realization of what is right'.) However, by the mid-1920's party discipline was not a matter of intellectual assent to party hegemony. The central apparatus of the party was deployed and the O.G.P.U. harried the rank-and-file opposition. By 1927 the apparatus of the party was able to organize unanimity within conferences and, as Schapiro puts it, 'a small minority, ruling by force in the teeth of the proletarian and peasant opposition, can ill afford to saw away the only firm branch which supports it—a well-disciplined organization' (1960, 308).

As with the Trotskyist Left Opposition the Bukharin Right Opposition put solidarity before all, and since Stalin controlled the apparatus of the party this played into his hands. But by April 1929 the Central Committee had accepted, as had the 16th Party Conference, the new industrial and agricultural policy, and the Right Opposition had formally capitulated to the party. Hence, the decision to eliminate the Kulaks (prosperous peasants), collectivize agriculture and speed industrialization could be implemented *via* a solid party. The Party was not yet the creature of Stalin—this occurred in the mid-1930's—but it was a disciplined instrument of political rule. The C.P.P. on the other hand was far less an instrument of disciplined rule when the period of maximum social pressure commenced in 1961–2, and never became so. Deutscher's characterization of the C.P., 'The individual Bolshevik ... belonged in his entirety to the party. He had no existence and no will beyond it', was in no sense applicable to the membership of the C.P.P. (Deutscher, 1966, 307).

This fact may have been a consequence of the greater intellectual coherence of Bolshevism, but it is doubtful since, although Stalinism means many things, it is difficult to see it as a body of deductive doctrine. On the contrary it was opportunism—or flexibility—transformed into a total 'philosophy'. Bolsheviks were loyal to the party and its historical mission, they can hardly have felt a loyalty to Stalinism *per se*. The most probable explanation, at this stage of the game, is also the simplest. Between 1917 and 1929 Russia was ruled by urban 'aliens', by foreigners who were a tiny minority of the population and who ruled through a party which in no sense represented the population. Bolshevism had to hang together or Bolsheviks were in danger of hanging apart. (As late as 1924 a peasant revolt in Georgia was an ominous sign of the possibilities.) The 1930's and the war changed this. Communism became the way of thinking, the norm of society.

Such was not the case with the C.P.P. It had begun, unlike the Bolsheviks, as a popular party embracing most sections of the population and only alienated its adherents gradually. It was, as we have seen, inspirationally urban but by no means exclusively urban. From the beginning its members had little hesitation in treating it as a ladder of upward mobility—to local or national office etc.—and if this proved unsatisfactory then there was opportunity elsewhere, e.g. N.L.M. and N.P.P. Loyalty was not, as it was in Russia, a matter of life or death. With its major object—independence—achieved, the party almost immediately fell back to consume the fruits of office. Again the C.P.P. was a mushroom growth in a relatively liberal environment and had not been hardened and bound together in underground struggle and repression. Similarly it had not shared, as had the old Bolsheviks, the experience of governing a destitute country amidst the turmoil of civil war and multi-invasion. And it was from amidst the confusion of these events that the Bolsheviks evolved *Cheka*—the political police—to control all the state institutions, bureaucrats and 'counter-revolutionaries' with an iron hand. No such organization emerged from the more liberal Ghanaian environment because initially it was not necessary, and when it was it was too late!

Quite simply the C.P.P. in contrast to the C.P. was a

blunt machette. Given time it may have become a sharp instrument, but Nkrumah did not give it time.

The strains of industrialization

This is an important point for one obvious reason: rapid industrialization *does* impose hardship on a population, and the more rapid the rate of capital accumulation—especially in basic industry—the greater the likely hardship. Such was the experience of Western Europe during the early phases of the industrial revolution. It is not a question of the political framework within which the change takes place. In France adult male suffrage and in Britain a very limited franchise hardly affected the fact of widespread misery during the period of primary industrial development. The resources have to come from somewhere—and normally the bulk is sweated out of the working population.

Economic growth in the primary stage is costly: 'It is because the economic and social costs of growth are so great and, in consequence, resistance to economic development is widespread . . . that a high degree of governmental control is likely' (Spengler, 1960). This was avoided in Britain because those exploited were weak, having neither vote nor effective bargaining power. And even so a growing measure of state intervention was necessary to curb the worst excesses. Politically the consequences of early industrialization are not far to seek: an alienation of the exploited from the regime. Naturally this is sharpened when the decision is politically inspired, centralized and easily attributable to a single authority, i.e. the State/Party. The process of industrialization then creates a hostile political environment within which the political élite must operate, and the environment naturally enough interacts with the political authority. Thus in

Britain some sort of accommodation, of compromise, was hesitatingly arrived at. In Russia the environment was changed, whilst in Ghana the political authority failed to find a suitable accommodation and was not cohesive enough to change and control the environment. The C.P.P. was not strong enough to manage the changes which it had helped to generate.

It is at this point that again one needs to refer to corruption and ostentation. The élite needs to be *seen* to be making sacrifices, getting to work and living at least only in moderate comfort. Two large houses, gaming casinos, expensive American cars, private swimming pools, free trips abroad, expensive marriages, imported luxuries, expensive girl friends, obvious parties—all of which flourished in Ghana—cannot but create envy and tension. Quite certainly the Communist Party on the whole differed from the Convention Peoples Party in this respect. If there was corruption it was relatively discreet and the leaders of the party, as a group, were ascetics by comparison with the C.P.P. élite. On the whole it is probably true that in Russia there was something like parity of sacrifice—some millions of peasants excepted—between the party and the people. If the party was a power or political élite it was only gradually that it became also an obvious consumption élite. This is true despite the fact that in the 1930's in various ways the income differentials between skilled and unskilled were far higher than was the case in West Europe and America. By the time the party became a party of the relatively privileged technical and intellectual élite, during the late 1930's the Soviet regime was firmly rivetted onto Russian society.

One further point remains to be made. Like Trotsky's view of history, forced and massive industrial change is not a taxi to be stopped at will. Once started the changes have a logic of their own and an impact on those precipitating the change. Like a river in flood, social and industrial change appears to seek out the 'weakest' and destroy it—and it strengthens the strong. Industrial revolution from above needs an able and powerful directorate as in the cases of Japan and Russia.

Industrialization under 'controlled' conditions is fraught with danger since it produces a technical 'middle class' likely to oppose the regime and a working class alienated from the system. Initial sacrifices are necessary and if, as was the case in Ghana, these sacrifices are demanded amidst a welter of ostentatious good living and political incompetence, the results are almost certain to be further tension. Hence a strong and disciplined political directorate becomes more than ever necessary. It is hard to imagine that an undisciplined and only loosely controlled Communist Party could have ridden the industrial and political flood.

It is a simple truth, but it is true, that even the worst regime can come to be accepted by people as a part of nature, but this needs time. During rapid planned social change it is one function of the party and the repressive agencies of the state to hold the people down, to gain time for the state to become 'natural'. Normally there will accompany the repression a whole range of resocializing devices whose function is to engender within the people, and especially the young, a set of attitudes likely to underpin the regime. But the inculcation of these new values and the growth of a new generation for whom the regime is a part of the order of things takes time, time that is purchased at a high social cost.

The decision to industrialize in Russia

Given the risks attendant upon speedy and forced industrialization, why did the two dictators embark upon such a course? Before discussing this question it is necessary to assert one simple proposition: any social change, or at least any radical change, is always accompanied by risk for the social and political élite controlling the country during the upheaval. *Laissez-faire* or centralized change throw up new social forces and bring about new social balances. Totalitarian and dictatorial control techniques, in this context, are thus substitutes for the risk-spreading typical of the uncontrolled change associated with capitalist or *laissez-faire* systems. And the control techniques of the one system are seldom completely absent from the other. Repression of trade unions, secret political police, foreign bogeys and system under-pinning ideologies (utilitarianism and nationalism) were not invented in Russia and Ghana. But if there is a risk in centrally directed change it would seem to follow from this, that those innaugurating the change must have had strong reasons for so doing, or they must have been impelled by circumstances beyond their control to take revolutionary measures.

There is little evidence that in either Ghana or the U.S.S.R. the decision to industrialize rapidly sprang inexorably from local political and social circumstances. This is *not* to suggest that rapid industrialization is a bad thing, or that the decisions were wrong-headed. The contention is that the decisions were not inevitable and that neither Stalin nor Nkrumah were the puppets of history. On the other hand, it would seem to follow from the previous argument that, having taken the decisions, certain consequences flowed from them. The most important of those consequences was the proliferation of social controls.

Concerning the circumstances surrounding the actual

decision in Russia to speed the pace of industrialization there is considerable argument. Deutscher in his biography of Stalin traces Stalin's vacillation between Left and Right, that is between a crash industrial programme based upon a grievously exploited population and a more moderate and gradual approach with the emphasis upon an accommodation with the rural peasantry, and especially the more prosperous *Kulak*. One thing is clear from his account: a peasant-based gradualist approach to socialism and industrialization was not, for a Marxist, unthinkable, since many Marxists actually recommended this course. Hence, one can dismiss immediately the idea that intellectually Stalin was up against a Marxist imperative. Deutscher, however, does suggest that 'Stalin was precipitated into collectivization by the chronic danger of famine in 1928 and 1929' (Deutscher, 1966, 322). But at the least this suggestion opens up the question of timing: if the danger was 'chronic'—and food *was* short in Russia from 1917—then why was agriculture not forcibly collectivized previously?

The heart of the matter would appear to be the fact that by 1927–28 industrial expansion on the basis of previously disused capital equipment was over and the available equipment was rapidly becoming redundant. Lacking any significant foreign credits—and with a peasantry consuming the bulk of its own produce leaving little for export or for the towns—only three courses appeared open. A more efficient peasant sector could be encouraged together with a more attractive policy of state farms, things could be left as they were, or, compulsory collectivization and expropriation of the peasantry could be undertaken. Solution number one was advocated but it did have obvious difficulties. It appeared that a peasant surplus was only available from the richer and larger peasantry and even the 'Right' wing of the party was not willing to face this consequence. Again, the voluntary principle, collectivization by agreement had failed and there was no no good reason to assume it would do better. The second alternative was unthinkable since Russia *was* threatened by famine. Thus there was little alternative, given previous government error, to some form of forced enlargement of the scale of rural agriculture. But this did not necessarily entail rank brutality, although it would quite certainly entail something between force and persuasion.

Another possible factor in the decision to industrialize was the widespread belief that Russia was virtually a country under the siege by the surrounding capitalist countries who would not for long remain content with a passive blockade. Stalin in 1927 made this clear; 'It can scarcely be doubted that the main issue of the present day is that of the threat of a new imperialist war. It is not a matter of some vague and immaterial "danger" but of the actual *threat* of a new war in general, and of a war against the U.S.S.R. in particular' (Stalin, 1954, ix, 328). In sounding the tocsin in 1927, however, Stalin was content to point to the divisions within imperialism and to the strength of the European and American working class as a real deterrent to an all-out war. But in a hair-raising survey of the elaborate preparations being made for the attack he reminded his audience of the need to stand firm and expose the designs of the imperialists. Only after this did he go on, almost *en passant*, to the need 'to increase the defensive capacity of our country, to expand our national economy, to improve our industry'. In 1927 then it is hardly likely that Stalin was thinking of industrialization as a source of armed strength against potential invasion. And even in 1933, in

F   69 his 'Report on the Results of the First Five Year Plan' Stalin actually relegated the defence aspect to the last of a list of its consequences: 'Finally, the task of the Five Year Plan was to create all the necessary technical and economic prerequisites for increasing to the utmost the defensive capacity of the country'. It was not until many years later that Stalin discovered that collectiviza- tion was really an imperative in view of the threat from Germany. In a general way defence may have been part of his reason, it can hardly have been the prime reason.

It can also be argued, more or less plausibly, that with the failure of the world revolution Russian Bolshevism found itself in a *cul-de-sac*: where to go from here. Stalin supplied the answer in his doctrine of Socialism in One Country, which by the last few years of the 1920's was received doctrine. 'What specific developments flowed from the doctrine? The answer in one word is— industrialization' (Kochan, 1963, 281). Now this view has much to recommend it, but it is subject to one crippling difficulty. Given that socialism, in its Marxist form any- way, inexorably points to a high priority for industrial development it is hardly credible to suggest that it points to the Stalinist model of industrial society. Stalin himself had said almost the opposite—possibly for tactical reasons —in his polemic with the Left.

The most convincing single reason for collectivization is that it was simply a control device over a peasantry that was untouched, or almost so, by the urban revolu- tion. It is possible to go further; in some respects Russia in 1928 resembled the dual power situation of 1917 with the relatively small but pivotal *Kulak* the real controller of rural life. This is the situation revealed by Schapiro: 'the better-off peasants, as the traditional leaders of village life, were the natural rivals of the Soviet administration which the party was endeavouring to build up' (1960, 338). And the failure of grain deliveries, due to the appetite of the peasantry for grain and goods (not available) was not a plot but a consequence of the sysem. Thus to attack the *Kulaks* was to attack a system in order to control it. Collectivization of agriculture was the imposition of the towns on the villages, the extension of control from town, to party to the country as a whole.

That the whole operation had a control aspect and was urban in its conception is obvious from the Motor Tractor Stations (M.T.S.) set up in 1929. They were urban mechanics, agronomists and technicians and were independent of the collectives they serviced, and it was only in them that the Communist Party had a substantial membership in the countryside. The M.T.S. were designed to control the collectives and 'assure the complete and timely fulfilment by the collectives . . . of all their obligations towards the state' (Jasny, 1949, 280). Each M.T.S. was in the nature of an urban outpost, a platoon from the town garrison.

Alongside collectivization went the drive for a massive industrial basis for Russian society. This was primarily financed, in its initial phases, by surpluses wrung from the villages. It involved hardships and suffering on a Promethean scale, and the erection of terror into a system of rule. Industrialism and industrialization put Russia through a mincing machine, a machine financed from the rural areas. Here was irony on the grand scale. The towns grind down the villages led by a party which was to be put through a machine grinding finest of all.

The decision to industrialize in Ghana

Nationalism, like socialism, in the underdeveloped countries contains within itself the seeds of economic development. Both can be regarded as under-pinnings of economic development. And in the Gold Coast/Ghana context economic demands—for a better standard of living—were stressed from the beginning and, as in the case of all modern nationalist movements, great efforts were made to cash in on economic discontent. In common with other nationalist movements the group around Nkrumah never failed to stress that the occupying power was exploiting the economic resources of the country for its own benefit. A glittering prospect! If only the money and resources sent abroad were invested in Ghana! Imperialism was purpose-built to keep the occupied country poor. Get rid of imperialism and economic reconstruction would commence.

The fact is that economic development was held to be an axiom, perhaps in need of definition but not requiring any defence. Debate on the methods and techniques of the process were possible, but its desirability was beyond question. This is clear from Nkrumah's *Africa Must Unite*. In this book he discusses in considerable detail 'the stresses and strains which have accompanied industrialization everywhere in the world', the shortage of capital, of skilled labour and everything else. But the whole discussion was predicated upon industrialization, 'the gigantic problem of transforming ... almost purely trading and raw-material producing economies into ... modern agriculture and industry'

There was also a political element involved in industrialization. Nkrumah maintained that an economically weak country would be a victim of neo-colonialist tricks and, more significantly, would be at the mercy of international price cycles. Hence, 'In planning national development, the constant, the fundamental guide is the need for economic independence'. Yet even as he was

72

writing these words in 1962 Ghana in fact was the victim of the dramatic drop in world cocoa prices.

If in the first period there was a gap between aspiration and actuality, nevertheless it is also true that the performance of the Ghanaian economy between 1955 and 1962 was not contemptible. Real Gross Domestic Produce 'increased by almost 40%, at an average yearly growth rate of 4.8% compound', and even if allowance is made for population growth, the G.D.P. per head rose by 15% over the period. Consumption too increased by 13% over the period, but a sharp cut-back in 1962 dropped the figure to the 1955 level (Birmingham, et al., 1966, 54).

However, something was wrong! Ghana did increase cocoa production from 260,000 tons in 1957 to 421,000 tons in 1962, yet earnings went up only from £51 million to £67 million. And its trade deficit was about 12% of available national product, yet little had been used to build up an import-substitute industry to staunch the deficit. Equally important, during this period foreign investment in industry in Ghana was minimal. Curiously enough it was only in the second period, when Ghana turned 'socialist', that private foreign capital inflows were significant! Most of this later investment was short term. In infra-structural development Ghana made progress.

But moderate success was not enough for President Nkrumah. Not for nothing was he the 'showboy'. And the show was not simply for Ghanaian audiences. Ghana was to be an example for the whole of Africa, it was to be a launching pad for Nkrumah's far wider political ambitions.

This suggests that the second period in Ghana, as in the U.S.S.R. did not spring from an ineluctable concatenation of circumstances which left President Nkrumah helpless. The decision was a conscious one, made in the full knowledge of the 'stresses and strains' which would be consequent upon it. Of course, none of this implies that it was a wrong decision. The contention is that the decision was conscious and that certain consequences naturally followed.

It was obvious in 1961 that the budgetary deficit of £31 million—which by 1962 was £47 million—did not constitute a viable basis for economic investment on the scale contemplated. Equally it is by no means certain that the stress on industrial development was sensible since Ghana was overwhelmingly an agricultural country which actually imported a considerable and growing amount of food! Ghana imported about five times the West African average in 1962 and only about 5% of the imported food was low-income type food. Just as important, a 1961 survey which proved that even in rural areas about 30% of the food consumed was purchased—not produced on a family plot—demonstrated the importance of a diverse agricultural programme. Something had been done to improve agriculture and diversify food crops and production, but food prices in Ghana rose sharply from 1955. This was probably due to a combination of inadequate agricultural investment, rising demand and inadequate marketing techniques, but whatever the cause the fact was that agricultural performance was inadequate. The balance towards heavy industry in the Second Five Year Plan and more especially in the Seven Year Plan was probably mistaken.

Mistaken in terms of economic efficiency and economic rationality, but not necessarily in psychological terms. Agricultural advance, even if spectacular, is not easily seen, but a mill or an electricity dam is. And after the excitement and furore of independence and its immediate aftermath comes the realization that almost everything is the same—except popular expectations.

We can tie in the preference for the policy of rapid industrialization with Nkrumah's political ambitions. It is clear that agricultural development would have been relatively unspectacular and would not have caused the stir that the more showy option did. And Nkrumah wished not only to impress his astonished African neighbours with the developments, he also wished, as he often emphasized, to lay the basis for regional economic development. Steel, aluminium and electricity from the Volta scheme were to be Ghana's offering for African economic complex. That this was the case with Ghana was made quite clear in the Seven Year Plan which dwelt on U.S. and Russian intra-continental trade patterns and set the Ghanaian plan in an African continental schema.

In turn this desire may well have tied in with the belief, evident in the 1960 White Paper on the Republican Constitution, that for practical purposes internal politics in Ghana no longer existed. Economic planning was an administrative technique requiring experts—which Nkrumah was not. He would devote his energies to foreign politics, and coming from a country as small as Ghana he needed the act of rapid industrialization in order to compete with the larger African countries. This was characteristic of Nkrumah. Stalin was almost a mirror image in this respect with his rather scanty attention to foreign politics related directly to his home problems.

In the following chapter an attempt will be made to examine the impact of these decisions on Ghanaian and Russian society and upon the parties through which the decisions were to be carried out. This will involve us in a discussion of totalitarian political systems.

4

Control: success and failure

We have explored some of the earlier social controls in Ghana and the U.S.S.R. and suggested that the C.P. was in a better position to impose further control than was the C.P.P. in Ghana. It is now necessary to examine the plans for economic development in the two regimes, the popular and élite responses to the impact of the plans, and answer the question—was Ghana moving towards the Soviet style of economic take-off? That is, was Ghana in process of becoming a totalitarian society?

Nkrumah's Seven Year Plan

The Seven Year Development sprang from the policy outlined in the C.P.P. document 'A Programme for Work and Happiness' and was accepted—but not initiated or meaningfully debated—by a party conference in July 1962. This document clearly stated the nation's goal as being socialism, which 'can only be achieved by a rapid change in the socio-economic structure of the country'. This was held to imply 'central planning . . . to ensure that the entire resources of the State . . . are employed in the best interests of all the people'. In line with the other developments discussed earlier the control and modification of the plan was not given to the Ministries, but to a State Planning Commission chaired by Nkrumah. The priorities of the plan, its frequent subsequent amendments and changes of emphasis, was the work of the C.P.P. politicians and reflected C.P.P. desires. It was a political and not an administrative document.

Total investment over the period 1963–70 was planned at £G.1,016 million, the bulk of which, £G.676 million, was from internal sources both private and public, with £G.340 million from abroad. Thus in one obvious respect at least, Ghana, although committed to socialism and an end of alien control, differed from the U.S.S.R. in encouraging both foreign and native private investment. Agricultural investment was to be £176 million whilst Industry, Mining and Transport accounted for £311 million; so again the stress was on industrial development. Both agricultural and industrial production was to increase, but the share of industrial products in domestic output was to increase from 23.6% to 27.5% whilst agriculture would decrease from 49.1% to 47.9%. Gross Domestic Product was to rise by the relatively moderate rate of 5.5% p.a. which amounted to a *per capita* increase of 3% assuming a 2.5% p.a. increase in the population.

The rise in population foreshadowed difficulties. It meant an increasing educational burden for a country with a young population spending a large amount on education. But it also meant that work had to be found for the school leavers, and the record since 1958 was not such as to warrant optimism. Just over 100,000 jobs had become available whilst 160,000 had left school. This was an obvious source of political instability and especially embarrassing for the C.P.P. whose support was primarily amongst the young.

Seen in the context of African development planning the Seven Year Plan was relatively moderate. The Plan depended upon external finances and internal private investment, yet the official xenophobia abated not in the least, and this was hardly calculated to inspire foreign governments or industry to invest on a long-term low interest basis. Failure in this meant that Ghana turned increasingly to short-term supplier credit, an expensive way of financing development. This in turn implied squeezing more from internal resources.

At least two major difficulties were encountered in squeezing more from the country's internal resources. Firstly, private capital formation in Ghana was small in relation to Gross Domestic Product and, therefore, unlikely to come up to plan expectations. Secondly, tax revenue in Ghana was inelastic relative to increases in income. Hence there was every possibility that Ghana would have to finance externally from supplier credits.

An equally significant long-term trend was inaugurated or, better, accelerated with the Seven Year Plan. This was the expected change in the social composition of Ghana. Increases in the 'high level' groups, including administrative (23%), technical (171%), professional (26%) and teachers (112%), were forecast. The total increase in this group was to be about 70% by 1970, and the 'high level' sector would be the most rapidly expanding of the nation. Following this group was the 'middle' level of clerical (51%), service (48%), semi-skilled (51%) etc., who were to increase by 51%. And although these groups were absolutely vital to Nkrumah's plans for a developing and socializing Ghana, only the semi-skilled of those increasing had any record of support for the C.P.P.

Judged by the scanty evidence available the Nkrumah regime was quite successful in recruiting teachers and personnel, but it was unable to get anything like the number of technically trained people. On the contrary,

78

and in striking contrast to the Russian achievement of the 1930's, the percentage of university students in science faculties showed a decline between 1957 and 1963.

In the African context the plan was a well thought out one and relatively detailed, although it was always possible to doubt the wisdom of the industrial emphasis, of the crash mechanization of agriculture and of the high level of social services. And the plan also depended on an export price for cocoa of over £200 a ton—in 1962 it averaged £163 a ton whilst the price of imports rose. But it was built onto an economy that although progressing was, in the words of an authoritative economic report in 1952, 'fragile'. Foreign reserves and cocoa prices had fallen, a wage freeze from 1960 coincided with rising prices so that by December 1963 real wages of unskilled workers were 81 based on July 1960 index of 119. In fact real wages for the unskilled rose from a 1951 trough of 65 to the 1960 high of 119, and from then on to 1966 real wages fell continuously. Wages and salaries for the skilled on the other hand moved upward, and international comparisons of income differentials between skilled and unskilled show Ghana to have one of the widest. Equally significant, the wage structure of Ghana was tilted in favour of clerical as opposed to technical and mechanical skills. Economically the plan then would have to depend upon reducing internal consumption of imported non-capital goods since export earnings were not rising and foreign private investment was not high enough to meet plan requirements. In turn this implied import restrictions and quotas—leading to the bonanza of corruption in granting import licences.

Import controls were in fact imposed in 1961. Thus the situation was that incomes rose amongst those sectors of the economy likely to demand imported goods, but their ability to purchase was restricted. In other words a form of forced saving and inflation was imposed by the control of imports. Amongst the unskilled, forced saving was imposed through falls in real wages, and amongst the cocoa farmers the same end was achieved with import restrictions, by a series of 'voluntary levies' and through the Cocoa Marketing Board which paid farmers about 52% of its profits. (Real prices for cocoa paid to farmers dropped from 200 in 1957 to 140 in 1963 — 1939 = 100 —.)

Stalin's Five Year Plan

The process of industrialization in Russia was to differ from that contemplated for Ghana in many respects, but probably the most significant was that Russia went without external help other than limited loans from Germany. The whole burden fell on the Russian people alone. Another important difference, connected with the first, was that Ghana was to remain a mixed economy with a strong state sector; in Russia the private element was almost eliminated. Hence in Russia the administrative burden of centralized economic decision-making—an astronomical task far beyond the capabilities of the Soviet bureaucracy—demanded a massive educational effort.

Stalin set the Russians a series of targets designed to transform the country into an industrial giant. Industrial production was to be raised by about 230%, the value of agricultural produce was to increase from 16 million to 26 million roubles and electrical power by 600%. The rate of capital investment increased from about 15% of national income in the 1920's to about 25% in the 1930's. (Ghana between 1955 and 1958 invested about 15% of national income in capital investment and by 1964 about 18%, but a great deal of this was from abroad.) Everything was to be massively increased except living standards, which by the best available calculations fell from 100 (1928) to 85 (1937) for the privileged wage and salary earners. Internal consumption was reduced to pay for the imports of machinery which rose from 24% of total import values in 1928 to 54% in 1932. Russia actually exported grain and dairy produce during the 1932 famine.

Real *per capita* income of the peasants declined by more than 20% in the same period (Chapman, 1963, 170). The result of the collectivization drive in the country was catastrophic, crops burnt and animals slaughtered (more than 100 million) but by March 1930 some 55% of peasants were on collective farms. Rural population was decimated (possibly to the extent of 5 million families) by deportation, by migration to the towns, by the secret police and by famine.

If rapid industrialization had meant only suffering on the scale just hinted at that would be one thing, but it meant more in Russia. Industrialization is more than economic deprivation, it is also induction from one way of life to another, it calls for a new set of values and attitudes to time. Industrial life is dominated by the rhythm of the clock and the machine and not by the time of the year. It is not without significance that Russia is now an important power on the world horological scene! Industry demands regularity and not seasonal effort—and industrialization was to come to the country and the town whilst at the same time the peasant came to town. Stalinism was not only an economic and political phenomenon, it was also a gigantic experiment in psychological re-orientation and mass 'education'.

Education, especially technical and professional, was very rapidly expanded by about 500% between 1928 and 1940 whilst numbers in general education slightly more than doubled. By 1940, Russian social structure changed fundamentally with a proletariat of about 32% of the population, bureaucracy, technical, armed forces officers and education personnel about 18% and a rural population of approximately 50%. This was in contrast to 1928 when about 13%–15% of the population was proletarian, 75% rural and the rest in bureaucracy, business, armed forces etc. Russsia had been reshuffled.

In order to achieve these results Stalin imposed upon Russia a political system novel in world history. Novel, not in the sense that elements of the post-1930 system were not present in the 1920's, or in the sense that elements could not be detected in other countries, but in the scale, variety and ruthlessness of their application. Stalin invented, or at least produced, the totalitarian political system.

Totalitarianism in principle

A great deal of debate and analysis of totalitarianism has been produced since the 1930's and explanations of its origins vary, but all agree that its essential function is social control and that totalitarianism is closely connected with terrorizing a population. In turn, it is agreed that terror in a totalitarian system is at root completely arbitrary in its impact; like rain it falls on the guilty and the innocent alike. It is, in principle, the opposite of law in a legal-democratic regime since law implies a measure of continuity and certainty. The totalitarian regime strikes at the root of legalism and for certainty substitutes uncertainty, for stability it substitutes movement and for existing forms of social organization it substitutes new ones. It also does away with a distinction basic to liberal civilization, the distinction between state and society, between the realm of politics and the rest. Render unto Caesar—everything.

Society is composed of groups, associations, interests and institutions and it is through these that people are 'taught' what is expected of them, how to react in various situations and what to value. Of these groups the most important and lasting in influence is the family, and it is the family to which the individual forms his strongest emotional attachments, and learns the primary 'lessons' of life. Probably the second most important source of political socialization is through the educational system of the country where national history, flag saluting, obedience etc. are inculcated into the young. Next in importance is probably religion, which normally teaches the young a divided obedience—unto God the things that are God's—although a politically subservient church, the Greek Orthodox in Russia, is not unknown. At the least the truly totalitarian society will wish to destroy or bring under control these three institutions, and any society which does not succeed is not for our purposes, totalitarian.

If these institutions are not controlled they constitute sources of alternative loyalty and opposition to the regime. They are *private* whilst the object of the regime is to make all things *public*. Hence the very art forms— heroic statuary, outward looking non-lyrical verse, march music—are public. The chosen weapon of the totalitarian system is terror and its function is to break up the sources of privacy by, paradoxically, initially making all citizens totally private.

Society is based upon trust, and the family in particular is so based; destroy the trust that people on the whole have for most others with whom they are in regular contact, and with it is destroyed the opposition to the totalitarian regime. Destroy trust and people necessarily are driven into themselves, and for most people this is

83

not the most satisfactory of journeys. Hence, the totalitarian regime does not only destroy, it also builds new and public institutions which may go down as deep as substitute family groups such as the party cell. The rôle of terror is to atomize society, to individuate it preparatory to or parallel with the building up of controlled institutions and, in principle, no section of the pre-existing society—least of all the totalitarian party—is exempt from terror. And the terror is not an accident or by-product.

Initially terror falls on real opponents of the regime, but during the second period, that of total social reconstruction, it falls on all sections of the society. It is arbitrary because the concept of *objective* guilt is removed. Guilt by association, group punishment, guilt through unpublished decree are common. Indeed, it is likely that in the final analysis totalitarianism is an attempt to wipe out the distinction between subjective and objective, between truth and falsehood. This is unforgettably brought out in the terrible torture scene in *1984* when O'Brien asks how many fingers he has in the air and Winston Smith correctly says four, whereupon he is further tortured. 'Two and two are four' says Winston. 'Sometimes, Winston, sometimes they are five. Sometimes they are three. Sometimes they are all of them at once,' replies O'Brien. Mathematics, the one certainty in a world of change, here a symbol of the rational and objective, has become relative and subjective.

Terror creates a situation in which loyalty to the regime can only be demonstrated, albeit temporarily, by denunciation by the self of the self and of others. 'It was no accident' that one official Soviet hero was the son who denounced his parents. That is, the basis of family trust is destroyed by the indoctrinated young denouncing the

recalcitrant old. It is the young who represent the future:
'We are the youth, and the world acclaims' etc. The
regime in the 1930's became geared to youth right up to
the top command posts, because it was youth that had
known nothing other than the regime and broadly accepted its priorities.

It is incorrect to talk of priorities in such a regime
in any very enduring or stable sense since they do not
appear to be ineluctably linked ideological imperatives.
The Nazi and Bolshevik ideologies did not give rise to
political or economic imperatives nor did they unequivoc-
ally point in one direction, or if they did the logic of the
ideology escaped both Hitler and Stalin. On the
contrary, their very certainty constituted a source of
instability within a totalitarian framework, the essence
of which is uncertainty. Nothing was stable and nothing
predictable. The relative intellectual coherence of Marxism
and the rambling edifice of Nazism were alike in this
respect.

In the totalitarian system ideology has other functions.
It is part of the apparatus of psychic disturbance. It
appears solid and knowable, but the closer one got to it
the more inchoate it became. But more important than
this is the other rôle of ideology, the creation of a verbal
pseudo-reality or the setting up of a public language
through which all experience is filtered and structured.
Phrases such as 'dictatorship of the proletariat', 'socialist
emulation', 'socialist morality', or, most dreadful, 'final
solution', when combined with a whole political language,
effectively blot out 'real' experience. Writing of Nazism,
Hannah Arendt explains that 'This outrageous cliché was
no longer issued to them from above, it was a self-fabricated
stock phrase, as devoid of reality as those clichés by which
people had lived for twelve years' (Arendt, 1963, 48). The

new reality is spread throughout the population from the party through its front or associated professional and youth organizations, control of the mass media, and by way of the educational system. It is this that was meant earlier when the 'Thirties in Russia was called an educational experiment.

Hence another feature of the totalitarian regime is the absolute control by the élite of *all* forms of communication including education, broadcasting, newspapers and public meetings. The object of this monopoly in the long run is to educate by completely restructuring the population's mental picture of the world by excluding any other interpretation for the old and re-socializing the young. In the long run this control is more important than terror which is possibly a transient, although vital, element of the early stage of the total society when most of the population was educated prior to the assumption of power. When the whole population is post-revolution, 'processed', terror may become old-fashioned and unnecessary, as may well be the case in the U.S.S.R. today.

Initially Soviet terror was exercised upon the peasantry and it *then* rebounded back into the towns. Managers, teachers, technocrats, scientists, officers, trade union directorates, in fact the political class of liberal industrial societies, are excluded from power in totalitarian systems by preventing the development of corporate consciousness, or if developed, as in Germany, by breaking it down as was done with the unions, the General Staff and the industrial monopolies. But if the functional groups composed of the people necessary to run a developing economy were excluded from political power, from any say in the economic or political priorities of the regime, they were a privileged group *vis à vis* the rest of the population. Wage differentials between skilled and un-

86

skilled, in contrast to the 1920's, greatly increased during the 1930's and this was encouraged by Stalin: 'we must draw up new wage scales that will take account of the difference between skilled and unskilled labour, between heavy and light work. We cannot tolerate a situation where a rolling-mill worker ... earns less than a sweeper' (Stalin, 1954, xiii, 59).

Totalitarianism is the political equivalent of having cake and eating it, the cake of industrialization and the edibility of élite control. Industrialization and political modernization always bring onto the political stage hitherto inert and dispersed social groups—workers and peasants—organizes them and educates them. Given a relatively liberal political climate these groups normally begin to have a say in the direction of their lives. And it is unlikely that they would volunteer to live the poverty-stricken lives of forced industrialization. Hence the control is exercised over the new groups, newly mobilized by the regime, in the name of the newest of the new—the future.

Totalitarianism in Russia: the purges

If labour was to be completely disciplined it was necessary to destroy the limited corporatism of its trade union leadership, and in particular Tomsky, who had suggested that some measure of real trade union protection was necessary. Condemned as a rightist at the 16th Party Congress in April 1929 Tomsky was dismissed, his followers purged, and a totally controlled trade unionism replaced that of the 1920's. The unions became nothing more than recruiting agents for the urban factories and disciplining agents for the state. Fluidity of labour, leaving a factory when conditions were bad, was abolished by December 1932 when internal passports were introduced.

Stakhanovism and socialist emulation, simply material incentives, were introduced a little later and were widely employed to raise the average norm of production. The consequence of this was that, in Deutscher's words, 'Russia [became] an almost classical country of a labour aristocracy'. Russia also became the land of the 'fixer', the man who at the risk of liberty undertook to short-circuit the bureaucracy and obtain materials necessary to meet a factory's allocated production quota. This involved all levels of Soviet management in illegality if they were to meet plan requirements.

The Soviet Russian army was the product of intervention, of Trotsky's multi-faceted genius and of the need to employ former Tsarist officers to form the technical cadre of an untrained force. It was in order to prevent a Bonapartist *coup* that Political Commissars were introduced to supervise the training and priorities amongst the soldiery. In order to do this the soldiers were subject to constant assessment of political consciousness and to political lectures and discussions, together with a bias in favour of urban recruitment which ensured that in 1933 some 43% of the army was of proletarian origin (Erickson, 1962, 373). The object of this was to keep the armed forces under the control of the party leadership. In the first of the 1930 purges, that of the 'Industrial Party' in November-December, the army was untouched. By 1930 the army was almost bolshevized at the corps command level, and about 70% of the army was in the party by 1934. And again in the 1933-4 purges the army was almost immune, but in 1937 Stalin struck and by 1938 the armed forces high command was almost totally changed and the lower ranks decimated. There was no risk of any army coup from those thus advanced and thus intimidated. 'Stalin had done himself a monumental service. Breaching a magic circle of the military, he had hurried the fractious, ambitious, independently minded or critical commanders into the oblivion of death or the N.K.V.D. labour camps' (*Ibid.*, 474).

But it was the dramatic purge of the party which demonstrated the rôle of purge and terror in the heroic phase of totalitarianism. The purge in the party was preceded by 'trials' of old mensheviks and of foreign industrial specialists, the former were convicted of plotting the re-establishment of capitalism and the latter of 'industrial wrecking and sabotage'. The first Five Year Plan was not going well and somebody *must* be to blame. The murder of Kirov in December 1934 ushered in the wave of purges which was to alter the structure of the party, beginning with the Right Wing of Zinoviev and Kamenev in 1935 and rapidly spreading through the party until nobody—except Stalin—was safe since the show trials of one group invariably implicated another. Accusation and secret denunciation became the only way of self-protection. It was an attack on the party and the object was to turn the party from an instrument of rule into a ruled instrument. Thus the new Party Statute of 1934 provided that 'periodic ... purges are to be carried out for the systematic cleansing of the party'. The eventual end of the purging process occurred when the secret police, the instrument of the purge, was turned upon itself and purged in 1938.

Estimates of the overall impact of the purge vary, but about 9 million people were arrested out of a population of 170 million, that is, about 5% of the population! Within the party the impact was even more shattering reducing it from 2.2 million in 1933 to 1.4 million in 1938, that is, about 45% of the party was purged. Every element in the party, especially the old bolsheviks, was destroyed as a basis for independent action against the regime. But if the old was utterly ruined the new was made by the purges.

Our country has entered a phase of development in which the working class must create its own industrial and technical intelligentsia' declared Stalin in 1931. It was this group that came to dominate the party, and by 1940 about 70% of new candidates for membership and new members were classifiable as 'intelligentsia'. In addition the party was becoming younger and post-revolutionary in composition so that by 1939 the majority of party secretaries were under 40 and had joined after 1924, and 70% of party members had joined since 1929. Not only was the party younger in 1939, it was also better educated with about 25% of conference delegates having received full time higher education as contrasted with 4.4% in 1930.

A significant ideological development also took place in Russia during the 1930's. Egalitarianism, which had played an important part in Marxist thinking, was shuffled off until the Stalinist equivalent of the Greek Kalends, that is until the arrival of Communism. Soviet socialism departed from the mainstream of European socialism which was, broadly speaking, more concerned with a fair distribution of the social product than with increasing it or, better, which assumed that the 'problem of production was solved'.

The changes in the composition of the Communist Party paralleled the changes in the social, ideological and economic structure of the country and the basic aim of industrializing the country was achieved. It was achieved at fantastic cost in suffering and with enormous waste of resources and it resulted in a rigid economic structure where duplication of effort was standard and waste built into the economic system. But an increase of basic industrial product of the order of 400% was achieved by 1940. Also during this period the peasants were broken as a real source of resistance to the regime. However, the single most important fact is that the regime survived and people came to maturity within it knowing no other: 'Each successive age group in the population seems to take the Soviet order more for granted', and amongst the young it is *specific* aspects, not general disagreement that sets them apart from the pre-revolutionary and post revolutionary generations (Inkeles, H. and Bauer, 1959, ch. 11). By 1940 the regime was stable.

Ideologically Russia had changed with the humanitarian and égalitarian elements of Marxism completely submerged beneath the dogmatic and rigid side. And this applied even to the language of philosophy and politics: It was as if the 'whole nation had succumbed to a ventriloquial obsession' (Deutscher, 1966, 363). Seen through the distorting lens of Stalinism the whole world became the enemy, fiendishly clever and capable of assuming a spectacular variety of disguises such as Fascism, Trotskyism, Right Wing Communism etc. And ideologically the nearer the 'enemy' was to Stalin the greater was his duplicity, hence the need for constant scrutiny of everybody's ideological credentials. Moreoever, the greater the progress made in Russia the more desperate became the enemy and the more insidious his attempts to upset the Soviet apple-cart. Thus Stalinism as an ideology came between him and reality and between the Communist Party and reality, both internally and in its foreign relations.

'Totalitarianism' in Ghana

We have seen that the wave of strikes in Ghana in July

1961 was followed by arrests of prominent 'old Bolsheviks' of the C.P.P. and further arrests and restrictions of opposition members. In December 1961 a government White Paper was issued which explained the strikes. It was inspired by the arrested opposition leaders, egged on and supported by 'certain expatriate interests', that attempts had been made to involve the army, that Togo, 'one of the countries where neo-colonialism has its strongest hold', was deeply involved. This looked in many ways like an amalgam of the sort of evidence that had inspired the Russian trials and the creation in early 1962 of a Special Criminal Division of the High Court to try crimes of a political nature caused some apprehension. In 1962 Ghana appeared on the edge of a purge. The P.D.A. was strengthened so that prisoners need not be released after five years. This was followed in April by an Act imposing draconic punishment for corrupt practices. Repression was stepped up in August 1962 after a bomb attempt on Nkrumah's life followed by the arrest of many recently released detainees. At the same time, Ako Adjei, a relative conservative and Foreign Minister, John Tettegah, the secretary of the recently formed All-African Trade Union Federation, Tawia Adamafio, the Minister of Information and H. Cofie-Crabbe, the party secretary, were arrested on charges of plotting against Nkrumah. The local press began to unmask a horrendous plot involving the U.S.A., West Germany, Britain and France to bring down Nkrumah. In September 1962 there was a series of bomb explosions in Accra. A state of emergency was declared and *all* ministers' houses were searched and, at the trial of the hired agents of the conspirators it appeared that the ripple was widening when it was disclosed that the bombs used were those of the Ghana Army and that Chief of the Defence Staff, Major General

Otu, was to be murdered and General Ankrah asked to seize power.

In the subsequent trial of the principal plotters, the government was concerned to establish that Busia and Gbedemah, both in exile, were co-plotters. However, and this happened in none of the Moscow trials, three of the accused were actually acquitted. The Chief Justice of Ghana who had presided, Sir Arku Korsah, was dismissed and all the defendants remained in custody. Whilst 'popular' demonstrations against the verdict were held the party press revealed a conspiracy against justice headed by one of the presiding judges, a blood relation of Gbedemah. The dismissal was also the sign for the press to demand a 'ruthless clean up in the judiciary, in the universities, in the civil service, and in the state corporations', but curiously enough the armed forces were not mentioned.

But the armed forces were not forgotten as Nkrumah made clear in September 1963 when addressing an officers passing-out parade. Stressing the need for discipline and 'loyalty to your Government and country', the President went on to say that it is 'important that you should identify yourselves closely with the ... policies of the Government and the aspirations of our party ... I am glad to learn (*sic*) in this connection that a Bureau of Current Affairs has been formed in the Army'. Direct and obvious interference with the armed forces reached a new high in June 1964 when a government directive ordered that the officers should enroll their men in the C.P.P. But the most dramatic intervention was in July 1965 when the President's Own Guard Regiment (P.O.G.R.) was removed from the army command, defence affairs were transferred to the President's office and the Chiefs of staff, Generals Ankrah and Otu were forcibly retired. The

H   93 army did not like this and after the coup Colonel Afrifa, one of the leaders, explained: 'Nkrumah introduced party politics into the army. He took a man with no training as an officer ... and put him in charge of military intelligence. Hence we had a situation in which mess corporals were watching commanding officers and reporting them'. At the same time all Ghana's top civil servants and officers in the armed forces vowed their unflinching support for Nkrumah's policies. The clean-up of judiciary demanded by the party press led to the dismissal of a number of high court judges. When the 'conspirators' were retried the judge was more compliant and the death sentence was imposed on all five, a verdict which was greeted with 'spontaneous' demonstrations against the 'vampires'.

In pointing out the lessons of the trial the press did not hesistate to declare that they had all *appeared* loyal and that 'As our socialist effort develops in scale and speed, the enemy within and without becomes more ferocious and cunning ... You must *demonstrate* your civic responsibility by reporting these to the police' (*Evening News*, Accra). In January 1964 the police chief was dismissed together with nine senior officers following a further attempt on Nkrumah's life by a police constable. Shortly after a referendum was held at which 99.9% of voters—101% in some areas—declared for a legal one-party state.

The overhaul of the university demanded by the party press was in fact part of a long-term campaign waged by the C.P.P. against the university which enjoyed a large measure of autonomy. This was gradually whittled away by Nkrumah who took the trouble in April 1963 to address the university on academic freedom and warn that staff and students 'must always be ready to expose those individuals in the university itself who abuse academic freedom'. The beginning of 1964 saw the most dramatic events with riotous C.P.P.-led mobs invading the campus following the deportation of a number of lecturers. Indeed, throughout 1964 the university and its Vice-Chancellor were harried and its books censored. The press throughout 1964 hammered away at the university and it is certainly true that the university did produce a majority who disliked the regime. It was in order to combat this that C.P.P. branches were set up in the universities, that students were encouraged to 'expose reactionary lecturers' and, finally it was decided that from January 1965 all new entrants to the university would undergo a two weeks orientation course in Nkrumaism at the party's Winneba Ideological Institute.

C.P.P. attempts to control youth did not end with the university students since the party aimed also at indoctrinating the very young through the Young Pioneers and those in secondary schools through the Young Peoples League. Both were established within the schools and both were evidently patterned on the Russian model.

Both of these organizations, of course, reflect the massive increases in the number of young Ghanaians receiving elementary and secondary education but who stood only a remote chance of further education. The resulting frustration would be dissolved in ideologically derived satisfactions. If, as was all too frequently the case, the school-leaver was unemployed—and Ghanaian development was capital—not labour—intensive—then there was always the Workers Brigade which taught elementary skills and advanced Nkrumaism. Unfortunately we lack any except the most indirect evidence of the efficacy of these organizations as agents of political socialization. It is known that the Workers Brigades had often to be disciplined, that resistance to the incursions of the Pioneers and Young Peoples Leagues into the schools was frequent and that a political career had a relatively low desirability amongst secondary school pupils (Foster, 1965, 281). These organizations were dissolved after the February 1966 coup without a murmur of protest. Whether they might have proved successful cannot be answered with certainty since they were not given time, and time was running out.

Economic crisis in Ghana

In 1963 taxes were again increased to take in those earning £11 a month, shortages of essential goods were obvious, and further import controls were established. In order to maintain level prices the government, in vain, imposed price controls. Prices in fact increased very rapidly —1963=100 and April 1965=145; but from April 1965 food prices rocketed. A new devil, 'the hoarder' appeared on the scene. He was normally a 'she', the market-women who had played such a large part in financing the C.P.P. in the early 1950's, but latterly known as 'domestic neo-colonialists'. Signs of obvious industrial and commercial mismanagement were everywhere, with very few government enterprises profitable or even well-run. In the first 1965 Budget speech it was explained that some £40 million had been invested in 32 state enterprises, only two of which showed profit; this was to finance a significant part of the Seven Year Plan. Government expenditure raced ahead of revenue and most of the deficit was financed by short-term producers, credits over which the Planning Commission had scant control or knowledge. Thus in 1964 Ghana had an external debt of about £187 million, of which £157 million was supppliers' credit, yet in 1963 it was thought that only £20 million was suppliers credit. Much of this credit had little to do with Seven Year Plan priorities, but a great deal to do with sagging British and West German exports from whence the credits were financed and the bribes to Ghanaian contacts paid. Most of these credits were due to be paid back from 1965 when Ghana would need approximately £24 million a year simply to service its loans from external earnings calculated to be about £150 million a year. Once again the farmers 'volunteered' a cut, this time of about 25% in cocoa prices in July 1965, and in September taxes were once again increased. As if this was not enough, the 1966 Budget further tightened exchange controls, introduced a 33% rent tax, further import duties and a registration fee of £50 on new cars.

It was in this situation that Nkrumah called for belt-tightening on a wide scale, a sentiment faithfully echoed —verbally—by the party. Yet most of the financial scandals and high-living involved influential C.P.P. members and government officials and their wives. In vain did the press hector and Nkrumah plead—from a sybarite's couch —for a modest way of life and ask them to 'accept a sterner discipline at all levels among Party functionaries'. Appeals to C.P.P. members to denounce 'opportunism' and to observe the party rules about criticism led to nothing more serious than the trials of a few minor functionaries and market-women. Ominous hints about reviewing membership and regulating the flow of new members sounded like the preliminaries to action. Yet again it appeared that a purge was on the way with the appointment of the Abraham Commission when the press once again thundered against the deviationists in the party.

As in the U.S.S.R. the heroic period saw the development of ideology from something marginally discussable towards a total explanation of everything. Ideological training for party members was constantly stressed in order that unalloyed loyalty to Nkrumah and Nkrumaism would develop the 'new type of man', a dedicated, devoted, modest and honest man. 'A man who submerges self in service'. Thus the constant stress on honesty and hard work and belt-tightening. But there was also a more sinister element of erecting a pseudo-reality. 'Ghana is the C.P.P. and the C.P.P. is Ghana' was not true since Ghana was a diverse society, but the party certainly attempted to make it true by bringing the country to heel. The frequent claims that, for example, 'workers are for the State and State for the workers, thus they are working for themselves', were simply excuses to take over and control the unions whilst denying wage claims. The country was beginning to veer towards one aspect of totalitarian reality, that is, the passion for unanimity with the 100% elections, the expulsion of opposition, the formalization of the one-party state and gradual calcifying of ideology. Alongside this process of intellectual *rigor mortis* went the familiar Stalinist claim to infallibility which was incorporated into the 1962 programme: 'This theory has been tried out in practice during the difficult circumstances of the last ten years. The progress that has been made is *indisputabe* proof of the practicability and correctness of the Party's line.'

The failure of Nkrumah

From about 1962 Nkrumaism seems to have entered a new phase of almost chiliastic urgency both in its internal and especially its external aspects. Whether this was a consequence or a cause of Ghana's growing isolation and waning influence in Africa cannot be known, but all along the line Ghana was failing. For example Nkrumah's

98

attack on the East African Federation in late 1963—as balkanization, neo-colonialism and the work of stooges—led to his isolation from East African affairs (Cox, R. 1964). This isolation was hardly mitigated by attacks in the press on 'the notorious Tom Mboya of Kenya, an agent of Neo-K . . . and a right wing fascist—preaching socialism' (*Evening News*, Accra). Similarly in inter-African trade union co-operation the Ghana-inspired All-African Trade Union Federation was merely one of a deluge of Ghanaian initials clamouring for African support and accusing, especially French African unions, of colonial puppetry. Again the implication of Ghana, through the training of men as guerrillas and in subversion, in the espionage in October 1964 in Niger, was one of the factors leading to the formation of the French-African Organization, *Commune Africaine et Malgache* in 1965. And this was quite clearly designed to counteract Nkrumah and amounted almost to a *cordon sanitaire* around Ghana. But the most dramatic examples of the isolation of Ghana was the June 1965 meeting of the Organization of African Unity called especially to discuss complaints against Ghana, and the refusal of other O.A.U. members to meet in Accra unless resident dissidents were expelled. Amidst all this Nkrumah published two books, *Consciencism*, in 1964 and *Neo-Colonialism. The Last Stage of Imperialism*, in 1965, both of which set out the ideology and tactics of Nkrumaism.

Both of these books are characterized by a demonological view of politics with world-wide conspiracies of ever greater complexity ranged against independent developing countries. Development is possible 'only through a struggle against the external forces which have a vested interest in keeping it (Africa) undeveloped'. The plot involved almost everything in the U.S. from Hollywood to the C.I.A. A new political language, closely based upon Marxism combined with a romantic African 'solidarism', was presented to the people and the party in *Consciencism*. But in his later book the tone changed and the African solidarism was replaced entirely with marxist jargon. The tone of both books is not one of the search for truth but of the presentation of the truth which, in *Consciencism*, can actually be reduced to theorems and equations. Who can argue with an equation? Whether intentionally or not the philosophic presentation bears the same relationship to philosophic uncertainty that the chapter on dialectics in *The Short History of the C.P.S.U.* (B) (1938) does to Marxism, that is inquiry has become redundant in the face of certainty. All that remains is exposition. And it was not a language of doubt or hesitancy, but of condemnation and action. It was this language which was to become the language of Ghanaian political life and especially the young of Ghana.

What the effect of this constant rainy season of words was on the people it is impossible to know, but the regime fell with few defenders. Its effects on the party are fairly clear, it served to isolate it from the people. Thus internally the party, which had begun as a mass party, began in 1960 a cadre of super-activists, the Vanguard Activists, to maintain party spirit and ideology. The influence of the party on the leadership had become nominal, as was the case in Russia, and it had degenerated into a claque of praise shouters—'Osagyefo will never die'. Nkrumah himself appeared more and more rarely in public and lived surrounded by the Presidential Guard. The country itself was gradually loosing its impact on African politics and this would appear to reflect the growing isolation of Nkrumah from Ghanaian reality. The country was buzzing with rumour and speculation about everything, in itself an indication that political communication between rulers and ruled was breaking down. People no longer trusted one another, Ghana had got into the habit of looking around before talking—or of not talking at all.

Over this shaky structure presided a party almost totally corrupt, as subsequent investigations amply demonstrated, and deriving benefits from the financial abuses on an heroic scale. Cut off from the masses the C.P.P. élite was in no position to reform itself and Nkrumah never reformed it, nor did he seriously try. Within twenty-four hours the structure of Ghanaian 'socialism' was toppled along with the statue of Nkrumah outside Parliament House. Those who had carried Nkrumah on their shoulders in 1951 carried pieces of the statue on their heads in 1966. It is a measure of the relative success of the two men that Russia had to await the death of Stalin before his statues crashed. Buses conveying the élite to gaol were greeted with delight, nobody raised a finger to help but many a fist was raised. The C.P.P. had exhausted its credit both internal and external.

Further Reading

The literature on comparative methodology is now so immense
that it threatens to engulf those engaged in the study; hence this
guide is necessarily highly selective. A useful starting point is
John Kautsky, *Political Change in Underdeveloped Countries*,
Wiley, London and New York, 1962, or Fred von der Mehden,
Politics of the Developing Countries, Prentice-Hall, New York,
1964. Those preferring a more abstract—and debatable—approach might try G. Almond and G. Powell, *Comparative Politics;
A Development Approach*, Little, Brown, Boston, 1964.
Although only indirectly concerned with the U.S.S.R., P. Wors-
ley, *The Third World*, Weidenfeld & Nicolson, London, University of Chicago Press, 1964, is immensely stimulating. D. Apter,
The Politics of Modernization, University of Chicago Press, 1965,
is extremely useful as is S. N. Eisenstadt, *Modernization: Protest
and Change*, Prentice-Hall, New Jersey, 1966.

A reading of any of the above, especially if some of the
footnotes are followed through, should familiarize the student
with the debates and discussions in the academic journals.
Amongst the most relevant of these are *World Politics, Journal
of Modern African Studies, Transition* and *Comparative Studies
in Society and History*.

Studies on various aspects of the U.S.S.R. of interest to the
student of politics are innumerable. Probably the best general
introductions are M. Fainsod, *How Russia is Ruled*, and W. W.
Rostow, *The Dynamics of Soviet Society*. All of the books
mentioned in the bibliography are useful on specialized aspects
of Soviet development, one not directly referred to but much in

mind is Z. Brzezinski, *The Permanent Purge*. S. Possony, *Lenin: The Comparative Revolutionary*, Allen & Unwin, 1966 and D. Shub, *Lenin*, Mentor, New York, 1965, are both highly readable.

Once again it is the academic journals, however that are most important for the student. *Problems of Communism*, *World Politics* and *Soviet Studies* are all very informative.

Although not written by a political scientist, D. Austin, *Politics in Ghana*, is the best introduction, but D. Apter, *The Gold Coast in Transition*, is more interesting methodologically. An interesting but somewhat perverse study is B. Fitch and M. Oppenheimer, 'Ghana : The End of an Illusion,' *Monthly Review Press*, July/August, 1966. Birmingham, Neustadt and Omaboe, *A Study of Contemporary Ghana* (2 vols) is essential as a contemporary reference work as is D. Kimble, *A Political History of Ghana*, Oxford University Press, London, 1963, for the period up to 1928. There is a growing library of general works on West Africa, two of the best are Ken Post, *The New States of West Africa*, Penguin, London, 1965, and P.C. Lloyd, *Africa in Social Change*, Penguin, London, 1967.

Most of the journals mentioned, plus *American Political Science Review*, *Political Studies*, and the weekly journal *West Africa* can be read with profit.

Bibliography

ALEXANDER, Major General H.T., (1965) *African Tightrope*, London: Pergamon.

APTER, D. (1955) *The Gold Coast in Transition*, Princeton University Press.

ARENDT, H. (1963) *Eichmann in Jerusalem*, London: Faber.

AUSTIN, D. (1960) *Politics in Ghana, 1940–1960*, London: Oxford University Press.

BIRMINGHAM, Neustadt and Omaboe (1960) *A Study of Contemporary Ghana*, Vol. I. London: Allen and Unwin.

BOURRETT, F. M. (1960) *The Road to Independence*, London: Oxford University Press.

CARR, E. H. (1950) *The Bolshevik Revolution*, London: Macmillan.

CARR, E. H. (1954) *A History of Soviet Russia*, London: Macmillan.

CARR, E. H. (1958) *Socialism in One Country*, London: Macmillan.

CHAPMAN, J. G. (1954) *Real Wages in Russia Since 1928*, Harvard University Press.

COLEMAN, J. S. and ROSBERG, C. G. (eds) (1964) *Political Parties and National Integration in Tropical Africa*, University of California Press.

COX, R. (1964) *Pan-Africanism in Practice*, London: Oxford University Press.

DEUTSCHER, I. (1950) *Soviet Trade Unions*, London: Royal Institute of International Affairs.

DEUTSCHER, I. (1966) *Stalin: A Political Biography*, London: Penguin Books.

ERIKSON, J. (1962) *The Soviet High Command*, London: Macmillan.

FAINSOD, M. (1953) *How Russia is Ruled*, Harvard University Press.

FAINSOD, M. (1958) *Smolensk under Soviet Rule*, London: Macmillan.

FOSTER, P. (1965) *Education and Social Change in Ghana*, London: Routledge & Kegan Paul.

FOSTER, P. (1943) *History of the C.P.S.U.*, Moscow.

HILL, P. (1963) *Migrant Cocoa Farmers of Southern Ghana*, London: Cambridge University Press.

HODGKIN, T. (1961) *African Political Parties*, London: Penguin Books.

INKELES, A. and BAUER, R. (1959) *The Soviet Citizen*, Harvard University Press.

JAHODA, G. (1961) *White Man*, London: Oxford Univerity Press.

JASNY, N. (1949) *The Socialized Agriculture of the U.S.S.R.*, Stanford University Press.

KENNAN, G. (1960) *Soviet Foreign Policy*, New York: Anchor Books.

KING, E. (1963) *Communist Education*, London: Methuen.

KLINE, G. (1957) *Soviet Education*, London: Routledge & Kegan Paul.

KOCHAN, L. (1963) *The Making of Modern Russia*, London: Penguin Books.

LEGUM, C. (1962) *Pan-Africanism*, New York: Praeger.

LENIN, V. I. (1947) *The State and Revolution*, London: Lawrence and Wishart.

LENIN, V. I. (1950) *What is to be Done?* London: Lawrence and Wishart.

LENIN, V. I. (1937) *Selected Works*, London: Lawrence and Wishart.

LYASHCHENKO, P. I. (1949) *History of the National Economy of Russia*, New York: Macmillan.

MAYNARD, Sir JOHN. (1962) *The Russian Peasant*, New York: Collier.

MAXWELL, R. (1962) *Information U.S.S.R.*, London: Pergamon.

BIBLIOGRAPHY

METCALFE, G. E. (1964) *Great Britain and Ghana: Documents on Ghana History*, London: Oxford University Press.

NKRUMAH, K. (1959) *Ghana*, London: Nelson.

NKRUMAH, K. (1947) *Towards Colonial Freedom*, London, privately printed.

NKRUMAH, K. (1961) *I Speak of Freedom*, London: Heinemann.

NKRUMAH, K. (1963) *Africa Must Unite*, London: Heinemann.

NOVE, A. (1964) *Was Stalin Really Necessary?*, London: Allen & Unwin.

PARK, A. (1957) *Bolshevism in Turkestan*, New York: Columbia University Press.

PIPES, R. (1954) *The Formation of the Soviet Union*, Harvard University Press.

ROSTOW, W. W. (1954) *The Dynamics of Soviet Society*, New York: Mentor Books.

SAUTOY, P. (1958) *Community Development in Ghana*, London: Oxford University Press.

SCHAPIRO, L. (1955) *The Origins of the Communist Autocracy*, London: Bell & Co.

SCHAPIRO, L. (1960) *The Communist Party of the Soviet Union*, London: Eyre & Spottiswoode.

STALIN, J. V. (1954) *Collected Works*, Moscow.

TIGER, L. S. (1962) *Bureaucracy in Ghana*, Ph. D. thesis, London University.

TIMOTHY, B. (1963) *Kwame Nkrumah*, London: Allen & Unwin.

WALSH, W. B. (1958) *Russia and the Soviet Union*, Ann Arbor: University of Michigan Press.

WALLERSTEIN, E. (1964) *The Road to Independence*, Paris: Mouton.

WARNER, D. (1961) *Ghana and the New Africa*, London: Muller.

WHEELER, G. (1960) *Racial Problems in Soviet Muslim Asia*, London: Oxford University Press.

Articles etc.

ADAMS, A. The Awakening of the Ukraine, *Slavic Review*, June 1963.

ERLICH, E. Preobrazhensky and Soviet Industrialization, *Quarterly Journal of Economics*, 1950.

Evening News (Accra).

JOHNSON, H. Economic Nationalism in Developing States, *Political Science Quarterly*, June 1965.

KATZ, Z. Party Political Education in Soviet Russia, *Soviet Studies*, January, 1965.

The Party (Accra).

RYWKIN, M. Central Asia and the Price of Sovietization, *Problems of Communism*, January, 1964.

SPENGLER, S. Economic Development: Political Preconditions and Political Consequences, *Journal of Politics*, 1960.

CHARLES II AND THE
CAVALIER HOUSE OF COMMONS
1663–1674

Author and Publishers are
indebted to the trustees
of
THE TAIT FUND
for a contribution towards
the cost of publication